42 States
of
Grace

42 States of Grace

A Woman's Journey

Maureen Hovenkotter

Gray Wings Press, LLC
Milwaukie, Oregon
2010

iv

ISBN 978-0-615-37162-7

Dedication

To my daughter Kristin and my son Karl:
Thank you for the privilege of being your mother
and
In Loving Memory of John

Part of the proceeds from the sale of this book will support the John Hovenkotter Memorial Scholarship Fund, the endowment established in John's memory through the St. Ignatius School Foundation.

vi

Introduction

*A journey of a thousand miles
begins with a single step.
~ Lao Tzu*

o paraphrase Chinese philosopher Lao Tzu, the father of Taoism, the first step in my journey of 25,000 miles was a year of prayerful reflection. This led to a decision in the spring of 2007 to set out on a journey to explore my country and try to find myself.

Life crises—losing a spouse, child, or parent; divorce; losing a job or even retirement—can plunge us into the realization that without transformation our life will crumble. The life crisis that led to my need for self-discovery and transformation was the accidental death of John, my husband of 33 years, in the fall of 2003.

After his death I faced nagging questions: What now? Who am I and what do I want? I realized the choices I had made as a younger woman were no longer valid, and I could not live an authentic life if I continued to blindly follow those paths, many of which had never been my true path to begin with.

While this major crisis was the tipping point, the bedrock of my life had been slowly undercut by doubts and confusion occurring over a much longer time. Little insecurities, defeats and surrenders, like water dripping on rock, had dissolved pieces of me until I had become a stranger in a life that didn't fit.

In the words of Dante in *The Divine Comedy*, "In the middle of the journey of our life I came to myself within a dark wood where the straight way was lost." I too needed to find myself and my way.

I had always lived in the Pacific Northwest, but I wondered if that was the best place for me. Would some other place fit me better?

For nearly two-thirds of my life I had been married, and I felt a strong pull to find another life partner; but this time alone could be a gift, an opportunity to focus on me, to get to know and befriend myself and find my true path and passion.

I had been a Roman Catholic all my life. My faith life had been a continual search for a deeper connection to God, though it sometimes felt like I took one step forward only to slip backwards. I wondered if a different spiritual path might be better.

I believe that the Creator, whom I choose to call God, is so generous, loving and genuinely creative that God would never limit us to only one right path. So many different people live so many different life experiences, are in such varied stages of spiritual development, how could God insist that we all follow the same path? I believe God is much wiser than that.

I also believe God delights in variety. Why else create so many wonderfully different people, so many beautiful places, so many amazing animals and plants? Life is an intriguing mystery, and we need to remain open to surprise and delight and joy. Closing off choices, tuning out God and each other, stops growth. Jesuit Anthony de Mello wrote: "On the day you cease to change you cease to live."

I believe God values our love and our creativity, our individuality and our authenticity and celebrates when we become the true persons we are created to be.

While my intent was not to run away, my decision several years after John's death to leave Portland for a time was also to heal from a broken heart. I needed to remove myself from the source of my pain and find time and space to learn to love myself better and try to accept the love God offers to all of us, unconditionally.

My decision seemed impetuous to some people, crazy to others, though many envied me this opportunity. Impetuousness and spontaneity can lead to regrets, but just as often they result in new discoveries and bold accomplishments. My decision to travel led to some regrets, but as time puts things into better perspective, I find awareness and new realizations have far outweighed any misgivings.

This book is the story of my coming-of-age journey, a pilgrimage I undertook at age 57 with my golden retriever, Charlie. While Charlie supervised, I drove a Class A motor home (a bus-like vehicle) through 41 states and one Canadian province, from north of Seattle to Key West, from San Diego to Bar Harbor. It follows the travels and travails of a single woman living the RV lifestyle while trying to find herself.

I lived in the motor home for more than a year, following my heart on several smaller trips before setting off on two major trips across the country and back. The first of the big trips began in August of 2007 and took Charlie and me across the northern part of the country to

Maine. During this portion of my pilgrimage I focused primarily on the interior journey, devoting more time to contemplation and prayer.

For the second extended trip, beginning in February 2008, Charlie and I invited a traveling companion, Keith, to join us in exploring the southern part of the country. Though I still sought prayer, introspection and growth, I spent more time exploring my outer world, giving this part of my story a slightly different flavor.

These travels and experiences made up my pilgrimage journey.

Most importantly, this book chronicles my inner journey, the story of my spiritual quest, finding my own right path to God, guided by a range of spiritual traditions. It follows the sometimes circuitous path that helped me come to terms with major changes in my life and helped me finally feel at home in my own skin.

The Catholic Dictionary defines *State of Grace* as "the state of being in God's friendship," and on this journey I often felt the peace and joy of knowing God was and is a friend. Grace itself is "temporary supernatural intervention by God to enlighten the mind or strengthen the will...a transient divine assistance" allowing us to grow in the life of God. During my journey I experienced what I considered supernatural intervention as well as unexplainable enlightenment and certainly a strength of will that I would never have believed existed within me.

I sought grace, though perhaps unconsciously, and found it in unexpected places and times. As I traveled, I realized that soaking in the beauty of creation, being mindful and present to it, and being deeply grateful to the Creator for such abundant blessings are graces in themselves and a way to thank God for such generosity.

We undertake pilgrimages for many reasons, but usually in hopes of learning something important about ourselves. In the foreword to *Traveling Souls: Contemporary Pilgrimage Stories*, a collection of modern pilgrims' stories Pico Iyer writes: "A pilgrim, ultimately, is a traveler moving toward the light, a light she hopes to collect and scatter across her path; where an adventurer may seek out a distant planet, the pilgrim only seeks the sun."

While my travels often sought the sun from a meteorological standpoint, my underlying hope was to bring enlightenment to my life.

Exposing myself to unfamiliar horizons and seeing new places with fresh eyes softened my heart, making it more malleable. I believe this openness to the unfamiliar helped me enter into places in my soul I'd never traveled to before. Exploring unknown highways gave me the curiosity and courage to let go of old beliefs and dogmas and explore new ways of seeing God, the world and myself.

A year after I returned to Oregon someone recommended *The Art of Pilgrimage: The Seeker's Guide to Making Travel Sacred* by Phil Cousineau. Reading it helped me sort through my experiences and guided me to new realizations from this time of journeying.

Cousineau's book helped me recognize that my journey was indeed a pilgrimage. He writes: "Remember that the risks you took, the physical and spiritual dangers you've encountered, the financial and spiritual sacrifices you've made, were to rediscover what is most sacred in your life."

Rediscover is key, because early in our lives I think we all know and accept the sacred, the mystery and awe of creation, the loving nature of God. It is only as we grow up, grow busy, listen to others and grow jaded that we lose sight of these truths. The deep wisdom of many spiritual paths resonates in our hearts, though we have a hard time hearing it over the noise and activity of our lives. It is what we all seek, perhaps unconsciously: a deep connection to our Creator, the source of all joy, happiness and peace.

42 States of Grace: A Woman's Journey recounts many of the challenges I encountered, the sacrifices I made, and the lessons I learned. Many of my new awarenesses confirmed vague thoughts and ideas I'd had since losing John; others were reminders of wisdom I'd trusted as a small child before life got complicated.

Cousineau writes that pilgrims must share the boon, the wisdom and graces received during their pilgrimage, with others who are ready to set out on their own journey. I hope my book can help and encourage others on their journeys, whether solitary weekend trips to the coast or longer journeys to places they've always longed to visit.

What did I learn? Come along on the journey and see for yourself. I hope my experiences will inspire other women of my age—the empty nesters, the sandwich generation with young adult children and elderly, frail parents to care for—to seek their own vision quests in whatever ways possible and ultimately find their most authentic self and their perfect place to be.

🌲🌼🌲

In writing of this journey, I have tried to protect the privacy of those who play a role in my story. In particular, I have made every effort to change or disguise identifying details regarding the men involved in the romantic relationships I include. I have shared only the details that are pertinent to my journey or that helped me learn more about myself. My experience knowing these three men helped me on this journey, and I thank them.

All the conversations depicted in the book are approximations of what was said, based on my very human memory. I make no claims that any quote represents exact wording or interpretation.

This is my story, no one else's. It is told completely from my personal perspective and reflects my opinions. There well may be other perspectives and other opinions, but I have tried to faithfully, truthfully and openly share mine.

BOOK ONE

Chapter 1
The Final Hours of My Old Life

I have always known
that at last I would
take this road.
But yesterday
I did not know
it would be today.
~ Narihira

October 3, 2003, seemed like an ordinary Friday until I heard words that would change my life beyond anything I could have imagined: "We can't stop the bleeding. He might not make it."

My husband John had flown to Yakima in central Washington State to help his elderly parents on their small acreage. John had loved growing up there and was happy to go back for a few days to help out.

Thursday night we talked on the phone and joked about just chucking work, selling the house and traveling. Both of us knew, however, that retirement was still a few years away. John was only 55, and I was 53. We needed to wait until I had completed ten years working as an aide to Oregon's U.S. Senator Gordon H. Smith. We shared "I love yous" before saying goodnight. John planned to be home Saturday to watch his beloved Washington State University Cougars play football on television.

Friday morning I had just returned from a meeting on housing issues when I received a phone call from my brother-in-law in Yakima. Mike had never called me at work. He never called us at home, for that matter, so my instincts should have been on high alert.

He told me John had been in an accident while driving the tractor on the upper pasture. When their mother went to check on him she found him lying next to the tractor at the bottom of the steep hill that divides the property. Mike didn't know the extent of John's injuries but gave me the phone number for the hospital.

I never imagined it was serious. It sounded like he had been thrown from the tractor. I pictured him with a broken leg or arm or perhaps a concussion. It seemed inconceivable that John might have stayed on the tractor and tried to steer it down the hill safely, that the tractor might have rolled over him as they plunged down. But in retrospect this is likely what happened that morning.

I called the hospital to find out how John was, hoping to talk to him. No one could tell me John's condition, but he seemed to be partially conscious though unable to talk on the phone. The nurse's questions about medications he was taking and other general health information didn't seem alarming. When I was finally able to speak directly with a doctor though, his words were chilling.

"His pelvis has been broken in about eight places," he told me. "He probably has internal injuries as well. We're not sure of the extent of the damage. He's lost a lot of blood. We can't seem to control the bleeding, and his blood pressure is very low, very unstable. We want to put him on a life flight to Seattle where they can better deal with the injuries, but we don't want to do that until we can stabilize him."

"Why Seattle? Why can't you bring him down to Portland?" I asked. "And what does this all mean? Will he ever be able to walk again?" Feeling desperate, I needed reassurance and certainty.

"We don't have a relationship with any Portland trauma hospitals," he explained. "And if we can't stop the bleeding, if we can't stabilize his blood pressure, he might not make it."

"Oh my God! Please tell him I love him." I had to relay the love I felt for my husband, who could be dying, through a stranger. I couldn't imagine John going through such challenges without me there beside him. I knew I had to get to him quickly, and if they wouldn't bring him to Portland, I would drive to Seattle.

After hanging up the phone, a dark shadow of fear filled my heart. I shared with a co-worker that "John might not survive the accident."

"Oh, he will, he'll be fine," Nancy tried to reassure me with a hug. "Don't you worry. You just go be with him."

I wanted to believe her, but the doctor's words were frightening. At that moment I realized my life would never be the same. Even if John survived, it was likely he would spend years in treatment and pain. His pelvis had been crushed. I doubted he would ever fully recover from the injuries. He would not want that kind of life.

Years later, I talked to Mike, who was with John in the hospital and flew with him on the air ambulance to Seattle. He told me then something I had not known: the doctors said John's veins and arteries were so badly crushed and mangled they weren't sure it would be possible to put them back together and have them work properly. They didn't even know the extent of damage to his organs; injury below his sternum was massive. Perhaps it was a blessing that all I knew on October 3 was that John was badly hurt and I needed to be with him.

I prepared to leave work, not knowing how long I would be in Seattle. I had called our daughter Kristin and told her what was happening. She and her fiancé Ryan planned to meet me to drive to Seattle. I asked a friend to take care of Charlie, who had joined our family as a puppy the year before.

I tried unsuccessfully to reach our son Karl by phone. I continued to try to track him down, leaving messages with friends for him to call me, while throwing a few clothes, toiletries and my address book into a suitcase and loading it into our red Mercury Mystique. I was on autopilot, trying not to think about the hours and days that might lie ahead of me, ahead of us.

Kristin and Ryan met me just north of Portland and followed me in their Toyota Echo. As I drove north I finally heard from Karl; he was already in Seattle visiting friends.

The doctor had told me John's flight would arrive at Harborview Medical Center around 3. Shortly after 3 I pulled over near the small town of Kalama along the Columbia River to call the hospital. Mike came on the phone.

"He didn't make it," Mike choked out.

"What? What do you mean?" I was unwilling to understand what he was saying.

"He didn't make it."

"What should I do?" I asked, not trusting myself to make any decisions. "Do I still come up to Seattle? I don't know what to do."

Mike had no idea, of course. He had just come through his own personal hell of being with his eldest brother as John fought for life and succumbed to death. But we agreed I should come to Seattle. John's sister Mary and brother Marty lived there. Karl was there. I needed family around me.

Kristin and Ryan had pulled off beside me. I tearfully told Kristin her father was gone, then held her while we cried. My heart ached for my daughter, who at 24 looked so much like her dad. She is small and slender: 5'3" and barely tipping the scales at 100 pounds, with fine, thin ash-blonde hair like John's. Her skills in organization, research and planning are among the personality traits she got from him.

I cried for Karl who would be turning 21 in 10 days. He still needed his father but now I would have to try to fill that role. Though he is nearly four years younger than Kristin, he had been taller and more solidly built than his sister most of his life. John had always called him "Big Guy," and was delighted when Karl's size, 6'+ and 240 pounds, and natural athleticism led him to play high school football. Karl favors my side of the family in looks and his quirky sense of humor but has his father's engaging, outgoing personality.

John had been incredibly proud of both our children who, in many ways, represent the best parts of us. In the years since his accident, I have consciously tried to remind them often of how much their father loved them.

On that disastrous Friday afternoon, knowing I was not in an emotional state to drive the rest of the way and contend with Seattle traffic, I left my car in Kalama and let Ryan drive. Much of the rest of the trip was a blur. Fortunately, Ryan had grown up in the Seattle area and found Harborview easily.

When we arrived in the waiting room, Kristin and I were comforted by John's siblings and Karl, who had arrived ahead of us. Then I asked to see John. I knew I would need the reality check, the closure of seeing his lifeless body.

Lying on the gurney was someone barely recognizable; so much blood and so many fluids had been pumped into him that his lean face had bloated, causing him to look 50 pounds heavier. His head was in a vise; blood was everywhere. I got blood on the khaki pants I was wearing, which I left unwashed and, inexplicably, saved with some of his things. It was a terrible way to remember the man I'd shared so much of my life with. For many nights that vision of John haunted me.

"Don't go," I begged holding onto his arm, already cold and stiff. "Don't leave me. How can you do this to me? Please don't die." I'm not sure how long I remained with him; it could have been a few minutes or many: time has a strange way of passing under such circumstances. Then I tearfully said goodbye to the man who had been my best friend for 35 years. I knew I was leaving behind the life I had known, and I had no idea what would come next.

As I walked out of the hospital with our children and John's family I didn't immediately recognize the dark figure staring back at me from the glass door. There stood a woman of medium build, medium height, shoulder-length light brown hair worn in a bob cut. In her khaki slacks and blue sweater she resembled me physically, but she looked so disheveled. So lost. She didn't look anything like the confident woman who had been chatting with a Portland City Commissioner only a few hours earlier.

How is it fair or right, I later demanded of God, that we were together for so many years, faced so many challenges together, but at the time of his death—when we most need and want loved ones by our side—I could not be there for him. That seemed so wrong. I should have been holding his hand, helping him, saying goodbye, and telling him I loved him. I felt cheated.

However, during those first days I also experienced feelings of trust and peace, despite my deep sadness. My faith in a benevolent God who cares deeply about all creatures reminded me God was by John's side even if I couldn't be. My belief that death is not the end, that we all can look forward to resurrection, sustained me. I was comforted that John shared those beliefs.

I didn't at all blame God for John's death. Most people struggle with questions of loss at some point in their lives. "Why did God allow this to happen?" It's fairly common to assume that God sends us difficult times to help us learn something, to teach us lessons, get our attention or even to punish us. Some argue that suffering in the world is proof that there is no God, or if there is, that God is unkind. Great philosophers have not yet been able to explain this adequately, though many have tried.

For myself, I don't believe God wants anyone to suffer harm, to lose loved ones, to be in physical or emotional pain. We are people of free will, and sometimes that free will takes us places God would rather we not go.

Life happens; accidents happen. Laws of physics say that when a tractor gets too close to the edge of a steep drop-off, it is likely to roll over the edge. If you are between the tractor and the ground, it is likely you will be crushed. Maybe it is an act of God's kindness that a life that would otherwise be filled with unbearable pain and sorrow be ended quickly. I held onto that belief.

As my pastor, Fr. Peter Byrne, SJ, put it once, God is the first one to cry and is there with us, holding us, when devastating events happen in our lives. During prayer and reflection on my loss of John, I pictured God as Michelangelo's Pieta: the grieving mother cradling her broken, beloved child.

At the same time, I believe God uses whatever happens in our lives to lead us ever closer. I believe God allows people into our lives to help us grow, to learn things we need to know. John had been a tremendous influence in my life.

I felt peace that John and I had tried hard to make our marriage work through challenging times and that I had tried to be a good wife and partner. At the same time, I was anxious about the ensuing years: how I would make it financially, what roads my life would follow. I could only trust my life would work out.

Back at home, holding onto his pillow, drinking in his scent as I tried to sleep, brought me a small measure of comfort. When I felt overwhelmed, I listened to the last voicemail he had left telling me he loved me, his voice a reminder that he lived on in my heart.

John had been a generous man with the soul of a philanthropist, sometimes giving more than his finances could support and occasionally sacrificing his own and his family's needs for others. He had always supported the Catholic school our children attended, so I set up a memorial scholarship in his name through the school's endowment fund. I talked with family and friends about an annual fund-raising event to support the scholarship and to remember John and celebrate his life. This seemed like a fitting tribute to him.

After a couple of weeks of feeling lost and trying to grasp my new reality, I returned to my job. It would give me something different to think about, other challenges to face that might be a little easier than sorting out my future. My work focused on housing, health, education, and other social issues, and I needed to feel that I still mattered and could make a difference. At the same time, losing John in such a brutal way helped me put some of life's irritations into better perspective.

Shortly after the Memorial Mass, Kristin moved to Vancouver, Washington, as she had been planning. Karl moved to Seattle in early 2004. Suddenly I had gone from a full house to just Charlie and me. My brother Tom offered to stay with me for a while to keep me company and pay a little rent. It eased my loneliness.

Tom was there to take care of Charlie when I went on my first trip to Mexico. John had always wanted to take me to Mexico in the winter. Shortly before the accident he had bought airline tickets for a trip in January to visit friends who had moved near Guadalajara. Knowing he would want me to go, I boarded the plane alone for my first trip abroad. It was not to be my last. I discovered I loved traveling and the warmth of Mexico beckoned me.

The following Christmas my younger sister and I went to Cabo San Lucas, Mexico, and it became an annual trip.

My brother stayed for three years and life continued, though not the way I had ever envisioned it. I kept trying to figure out why this had happened, to make some sense of this loss. Was there something God wanted me to do now that John was no longer in my life? These questions led me on a search for purpose, a search for God, and, ultimately on a journey in search of myself.

Chapter 2
The Real Journey Begins

It may be that when we no longer know what to do
we have come to our real work,
and that when we no longer know which way to go
we have come to our real journey.
~ Wendell Berry

Following John's death as I continued working for the U.S. Senate I realized I had a limited view of my country. I had seen much of the West and had visited Washington, D.C. and Boston on business. The rest of the country I had been serving was a mystery I wanted to unravel. I wanted to experience the varied cultures, talk to people who looked at life differently.

Being alone for the first time in my life had forced me to stretch and grow, to make my own decisions. It was no longer a shared life; it was my life, and I could choose to live it any way I wanted. This was incredibly freeing yet also incredibly frightening. I had few clues about who I was and how I wanted to spend what was left of my life. I needed time and space to find those answers.

I also needed time to heal. In October 2004, my father passed away. He had been a strong and loving presence in my life. My mother had died of breast cancer eight years earlier. Kristin moved from Vancouver to Coos Bay, Oregon, several hours away. I had only my brother and Charlie.

And for 15 months I had Lance, a man I thought was a gift from God. But in July of 2005, Lance took that gift away and broke my heart. My sense of my place in the world and my self-worth were shattered. I felt like I'd lost my anchor and was drifting aimlessly.

In September of 2006 I enrolled in a group retreat following the Spiritual Exercises of St. Ignatius to discern my next steps in life. Normally conducted as a 30-day intensive retreat, SEEL stretches this experience of deepening one's relationship with God and developing spiritual discernment skills over nine months. I hoped to find inspiration, to discover God's will for me. As the retreat proceeded, I became convinced that I needed to do something radically different. My life was stagnant. Something was missing, and I often felt that I was just going through the motions.

In March of 2007 I would reach the important ten-year mark on my federal job. I was 56 and would qualify to retire with medical insurance. The nearer it got, the more I thought about it.

Losing my mother at the age of 69 from breast cancer and then my husband at the age of 55 were grim reminders to live life while I had it. I had the freedom to do something completely different than I'd ever done, though I still wasn't sure what that would look like. If I pared down my expenses, I thought I might be able to find the time and inspiration I needed to move my life forward on a different road.

Paring down expenses would be tricky. The split-entry home John and I had built in Southeast Portland in 1993 was increasing in value as the neighborhood gentrified and became popular. My adjustable rate mortgage had just increased and my property taxes were becoming prohibitive. I didn't think I could afford to stay there if I retired.

The idea of traveling, being rootless, a vagabond, had often pulled at me, and the open road continued to beckon. I thought perhaps I could live within my means if I sold the house, sold or got rid of most of my possessions, bought a motor home and lived in it.

In the back of my mind was the dream John and I had to retire early and explore the United States together. We had shared this dream after several very challenging years that nearly split our marriage apart. When he died, I packed that dream away in the old steamer trunk his great-grandfather had brought from Germany, along with other mementos of John, believing it was something I could never do alone. But the dream was still there waiting for me to come to my senses and rediscover it. A persistent voice kept whispering to me: You can do this; don't be afraid.

I often stew over decisions for weeks or months, letting them percolate, tasting them in my mind. But once I have decided to move forward, I don't like to be bothered by details, plotting and planning, research, or reading directions. Those were all things John loved, and I was happy to leave them to him. When the time seems right to do something, I want to start NOW. Sometimes the tipping point is as simple as listening to a friend.

While I was mulling over whether I wanted to—and could—do this traveling, one night I had a glass of wine with my hair stylist Fran. She is a breast cancer survivor and her husband was fighting congestive heart failure at the time.

"Do it. I would if I could," she encouraged me. "Never pass by a chance to live your life, to find adventure. You never know how this will change your life, and you'll always wonder if you don't do it."

That was all the encouragement I needed; I knew I had to do something, and this seemed right. Perhaps this was God's message, an angel speaking through a friend to help me decide.

The next day I gave my retirement notice and began planning my adventure. I made plans to sell the house and furniture, go through all the files and shred almost everything, find an appropriate motor home, research RV camping organizations, learn more about bio-diesel, and plot out the trip.

I made plans to meet my younger sister Shirley in early August at her home in Minnesota to accompany her on her dream of canoeing the Boundary Waters. From there I thought I would continue east, planning to be in New England for the fall colors, and then wherever the wind and inspiration blew me.

To share my travels with family and friends, I set up a blog: www.travelinwithCharlie.com. It was appropriate to give Charlie credit because he had a role in this decision, albeit a silent one.

Charlie is a lovely retriever, a rich golden color with a funny little black spot on his tongue that wasn't there until he was close to a year old. He weighs about 85 pounds and has a deep, threatening bark, which he usually reserves for cats or squirrels. I doubt if he would ever harm a human; he thinks they're all put on this earth to be his friend, throw the ball for him, pet him, feed him treats and adore him.

John and I had owned a golden retriever years earlier. Murphy came to us as a stray. We didn't know his age or history, though he was not young and had broken off most of his teeth. We loved his personality and promised ourselves when he passed away that we would some day own another golden.

For John's 54th birthday, July 4, 2002, I decided it was time. Following up on an ad in the paper, we drove far out into the country to see a litter of 12 beautiful puppies. After playing with them for more than an hour, I had settled on a large, blonde male.

"We'd better choose one. Here's the one I like." I held up the squirming ball of golden fur. "What about you?"

"That one's fine but we're obviously not going home without this one." John pointed to his feet. A puppy was leaning against his leg possessively. He wasn't the runt, but probably next in line. He had spots on his leg and hip from ringworm. Accepting there was a reason this puppy had selected us, and knowing we couldn't afford two, I agreed.

"What are we going to name him?" John wondered as he drove home and I held the puppy snugly on my lap.

For some reason I thought of my grandfather whom we had visited in Arizona a couple of times. His name was Charles; everyone called him Chuck except John, who called him Charlie.

"How about Charlie?" With that suggestion Charlie became part of our lives.

We'd both grown up with dogs but had never raised a puppy. What an experience! He chewed holes in the sofa, he chewed holes in shirts and towels. One day he even chewed a hole in the sheetrock wall. We learned to provide a variety of chew toys for him. To this day he still likes to have something in his mouth when he's excited.

Charlie loved to go for rides in the car, as well as long walks. Watching him run ahead of us as we walked on park trails was to see grace and beauty and energy working together. His demeanor was sheer ecstasy, unrestrained joy.

Charlie grew to be a beautiful and affectionate dog. He loved people, he loved attention, and he worshiped John. When John never returned the following October, Charlie kept waiting and watching for his beloved master to come home. His disappointment was palpable. He lay with his head on his paws, his normal joy in life gone. As the weeks and months went by, we provided solace for each other; sometimes I would wrap my arms around his neck and sob into his fur, crying for him, for me, for our lost future.

I envisioned this trip as an extended joy ride providing me plenty of time to shower Charlie with attention and love.

🌲🌺🌲

In the weeks after announcing my retirement I found myself in a flurry of activity that kept me from having many second thoughts about my decision to retire and travel. Those would come later.

I purchased a 2002 36-foot Monaco motor home, which I dubbed the Mo, and spent an afternoon with the previous owner learning to operate it. I made a couple of short trips to test out my driving skills and practice setting up the Mo. Despite my lack of knowledge about the lifestyle, I forged ahead, confident I would find the necessary skills and knowledge when I needed them.

I went through a lifetime of accumulated possessions and scheduled an estate sale, which earned me a disappointing $1,500. This reminded me that possessions are only worth the momentary enjoyment they bring. You exchange part of your life—the time you spend working—to purchase things that will likely never have value beyond the immediate pleasure they provide. If they add beauty to life, create an environment that enhances happiness and peace, then perhaps they are worth it. This wisdom can guide future decisions of when and where to spend my money and reminds me to appreciate things I buy.

I am becoming more aware that possessions, power or reputations are not what matter in life; it is relationships—with those we love, ourselves, our Creator and all of creation—that are important. If our relationships aren't healthy, possessions will never fill the emptiness.

Offsetting my financial losses, the weekend of the estate sale I held a blessing ceremony for the Mo and the journey. It was wonderful to gather with friends before beginning my travels; family and friends are the true riches in my life, and I knew I would miss them.

By mid-May I had moved into the Mo while waiting for my house to sell. I was hoping to get it sold quickly since prices were already slipping in the Portland market. When I didn't need to be in Portland to meet some final commitments or sign papers on the house, I spent time on the Oregon and Washington coasts.

The more I drove the Mo, the more comfortable and natural it became. Despite some frustrations when I tried to hook up to electric, water and sewer on my first trip and couldn't get anything to work, I soon became adept at it and able to set up camp in a matter of minutes.

🌲 🌼 🌲

I discovered I could not tow the Toyota RAV4 I had purchased several months after John died, so I loaned it to Karl, who had married and returned to the Portland area, and I began looking for a car for my cross-country trip.

One morning I was sitting in the clubhouse at an RV park on the Oregon coast when a rig pulled in towing a dinghy with a "for sale" sign on it. It was a cute, red sporty Saturn, which make excellent dinghies. I talked to the woman, Bev, who said they had just decided to sell the car that morning before leaving their home in Southwest Washington. It came with all the towing equipment, which was exactly what I had been looking for. In my conversations with Bev and her husband, Gary, I learned that he had grown up in Yakima and been friends with one of John's uncles. We agreed on a price and a date for me to pick the Saturn up at their home east of Vancouver.

"You know, it was real last minute that we even brought the car," Bev said. "I'm not sure why we decided to hook it up and bring it."

"I know why you brought it," I said handing her a deposit check. "You were supposed to be here with it because I need a car. I've had too many of these coincidences lately to not realize there's more at work here than mere chance."

🌲 🌼 🌲

Charlie and I spent leisurely days walking on the beach or exploring small beach towns. Our walks revealed blooming wild rhododendrons in varying shades of pink and coast iris, orchid-colored beauties only about six inches tall. Scotch broom, lupine and other wildflowers bloomed abundantly among ferns and salal.

One morning we walked the beach just after sunrise. It was glorious—no one else around; our footprints were the first on virgin sand. Every time the tide comes in, it washes the sand clean and the beach is once again left pure, untouched.

I thought about how often in life I wished for a "do-over," for a clean canvas. Maybe those opportunities were there if I took the time to recognize them, reach out and grasp them. Maybe it just required getting off the treadmill and stepping out onto the sand, being willing to get my feet wet, looking out at the vast and ever-changing ocean and realizing life is truly beautiful and abundantly rich in opportunities, forgiveness and do-overs. I felt gratitude this early retirement allowed me to experience scenes I would have otherwise missed in my rush through life.

One day while relaxing on a sun-filled beach I watched as Charlie tried to catch seagulls. As he dashed madly after them, they easily escaped.

"Charlie!" I called him over and petted him, then winced as he shook, showering me with sand and water. "You'll never be able to run as fast as they can fly. You need to sneak up on them. Or just lie quietly and wait and they won't even notice you. Then they'll wander close enough so maybe you can at least have a chance."

He smiled at me, his pink tongue lolling out between his sharp teeth. *Right, why didn't I think of that? You're so smart, Mom!* Then he turned and ran back down towards the waves rolling onto the sandy beach. He ran in circles just for the joy of being a dog in his natural element. His playfulness and exuberance were contagious, and I laughed in appreciation at his antics.

As I watched Charlie run off-leash, unencumbered, I experienced another lesson in being authentic. I wondered what shackles keep me from being free, from living my own true life. One is fear—of the future, of criticism, of failure, of not fitting in. What if I could let myself off the leash? What adventures could I discover? What joy?

I know Charlie doesn't understand the concept of waiting and letting life come to him. It is ingrained in dogs to go out searching for food, especially when they see it within a few leaps. I wondered if my decision to sell everything and set out on this journey was a rash attempt to chase answers that seemed as elusive as the seagulls. Or was I acting on a prompt—from God or from myself—to find a little more freedom in my life. I was convinced my recent actions were designed to give myself the gift of being still and silent and lie in wait for food for my soul, to just wait for God.

The night before, while searching for something else, I came across notes I had written years before while on retreat just south of here. I had been sitting for some time in the middle of a big meadow with a view of the bay. Another woman from the retreat came walking up the dirt road that bisected the field. She didn't see me. She also didn't see the doe that stood nearby watching her. The doe had no idea I was there. It was fascinating. As I sat there waiting, life came to me, and I felt and understood God's presence.

I thought about that experience and wondered about this in-between time. Though I hadn't yet set off for any far destinations, it was still important time. I had no expectations or deadlines pulling at me, no routes to plot out. I could focus on the interior journey that called to me. I realized this might be the only way I would find what I was looking for: by being still, by waiting, by letting God.

This was a time to learn to be alone, to deal with challenges without help from family or friends. It was a time for reflection and introspection about myself and what I hoped to accomplish.

I often felt frustrated and confused. I sensed that I was standing with a foot in two different worlds: my old life and friends, my old house and things, and a new life that was still mostly unformed and as unfocused as the coastal landscape in heavy fog. I felt like a refugee: displaced, rootless, lost.

My conversations with God were filled with frustration, and pain—and plenty of questions about what this was all for. I believed I was doing what I had been asked to do for the time being: give up everything and step out in faith. And I had surrendered a lot: security, friends, roots, routine, comfort, all my things; my faith community and the support from that; the status and influence I had as an aide to a Senator. I felt not only lost but naked, without protection, subject to whatever the winds blew my way. And I felt utterly devoid of a cause, of a mission, of some sense that I was doing anything to make a difference in the world.

Part of me wanted my life to go back to the way it was, with my friends, my house, my things and even my job still intact. But I knew that my life would never be as it had been before John was killed, before my children moved away from home and on with their lives. I had to face that reality and put some distance between myself and that old life to get a better perspective on new possibilities that could be waiting if I had the courage to break free and be open to them.

As I continued to struggle with the changes in my life, I often found messages in natural phenomena—unexpected gifts and blessings seemed to appear when I most needed them.

One morning all along the beach I found crumpled shells: little pieces of sand dollars, clam and mussel shells, some so small there was no way to know what they came from. They had been battered by the ocean, smashed by the rocks. And yet there was still beauty in them. I picked up a small piece that had lines of pearlescence in it.

I thought about the trials and struggles everyone goes through. Though we may feel we have been broken beyond repair and believe there is no value or beauty left in us, there is still much to be admired, appreciated and loved. All these pieces of broken shells together added interest, personality and texture to the beach just as all of us in our brokenness add beauty and variety to each other's lives. Being broken means you are different, you don't fit into that perfect mold of "normal" so many aspire to. You can understand and resonate with the brokenness of others; you can feel their pain because you have felt your own so deeply. Being broken expands your capacity for compassion and understanding.

꙳

Chapter 3
Goodbye to Yesterdays

Say goodbye
To golden yesterdays
—or your heart
will never learn
to love
the present.
        ~ Anthony de Mello, SJ

It is late May, and I feel pulled to begin my journey and start separating from my life in Oregon. I still have obligations in Portland that prevent me from embarking on an extended trip, but it feels like time to step outside my comfort zone and begin driving unfamiliar highways.

I have decided to travel to Polson, Montana, to visit John's brother Joe and his family. I invite their mother Marian to join me. She has been a widow since John's father Larry died the previous October after a long bout with Parkinson's. My invitation is offered in support of her loss and also in an attempt to heal old wounds.

Following John's accident, my relationship with Marian had become strained over some financial issues. I wanted to file a claim against their homeowner's insurance for John's death. Kristin had finished college but was saddled with huge student loans we had hoped to help with. Karl did not have the money to attend college. I hoped an insurance settlement would help make up for the loss of their father's income. Most of the family agreed, but Marian made some misleading statements to the insurance investigator that resulted in the claim being denied. I was furious. Joe, an attorney, had tried to help but Marian's statements were too damaging.

I've held this resentment in check, buried but still there, for more than three years. I know John would want me to deal with that anger and try to put it behind me. I hope our time together will allow us to talk about our disagreements and find peace again. Alternatively, I figure I can always just drop her along the road somewhere.

On the Tuesday before Memorial Day I drive to Yakima to meet Marian. I pull into in her driveway and use my hydraulic jacks to level the Mo. It still isn't level according to my gauge so I lower the left jack more, but it doesn't help. I check under the Mo and discover the jack has drilled a 6-inch hole through the pavement. Thinking the pavement is thin in this spot, I move the rig over a couple feet and try to level again. Later I discover the jack has drilled another hole. I move the Mo a third time, putting pieces of lumber under the jacks to spread the weight, which seems to work.

During the drive to Yakima my bicycle had been bouncing precariously on the back of the Mo. On Wednesday my brother Michael, who also lives in Yakima, meets me. We shop for a rack, then he installs it and ties my bike down more securely while Marian packs her clothing and personal items.

Thursday morning we leave Yakima and drive on dry roads through sunshine across central and eastern Washington. Just west of Spokane it begins to rain, and we drive through rain, thunder and lightning across the Idaho Panhandle and Western Montana. Marian has never cared much for dogs, but she is a good sport and spends much of the trip petting Charlie, allowing me to focus on driving without having to fend off his need for constant attention.

🌲🌼🌲

"John would have absolutely loved this." I am standing next to Joe gazing down on the breathtaking view of Flathead Lake, dotted with islands. Joe and his wife Roxanne own 110 acres on the hills overlooking Polson. "He always wanted to come see your place."

We arrived about an hour ago, finally getting a break in the rain and storms. Joe and I watch the sunset cast a mauve glow on everything it touches. Gazing out at the silver-blue expanse of lake and the mountains, I have a deep sense of peace and of God's presence in my life. John, indeed, would have loved it.

Some 15 years earlier, on our way to Glacier National Park, we spent two nights in Big Fork on the east side of Flathead Lake. It was one of several trips we took with the children when we owned a travel trailer. Years before, when Kristin was three and I was about seven months pregnant with Karl, we had visited Bozeman and Yellowstone National Park.

As Joe and I talk, we turn to see the snow-crowned Mission Mountains to the east, glowing pink in the dusk. Meadowlarks call to each other in the tall grass covering the surrounding hills. A fox barking in the distance catches Charlie's attention, and he pauses his sniffing explorations to listen.

This truly is inspiring country, with a wild rawness that invokes awe and respect. The jagged peaks of the surrounding mountains, marching off into the misty distance in all directions, promise a challenging life.

"Winters can be brutal here," Joe reminds me as I admire the abundant beauty. "Sometimes we get socked in with clouds and fog and don't see the sun for days at a time."

"Sounds like Portland or Seattle." I pull my windblown hair back out of my face, one of the downsides of long, thick hair. "I figured Montana would have sunny, crisp winter days like we had in Yakima. You know, blue skies and sun but that biting cold that makes your nostrils freeze together when you inhale. "

"Well, the cold part is right."

Exhausted from the ten-hour drive fighting wind and rain, I head for bed. We are boondocking or "dry camping," running off the batteries and generator, which I have finally figured out how to start. We have no sewer connection and are using the water from my tanks. To avoid overfilling my blackwater tank, we will use one of the bathrooms in the house and eat most of our meals with Joe and Rox and their three children.

We spend Friday visiting and catching up and drinking in the beauty of this place. Down the hill from the house a family of coyotes has established their den. In the warmth of the afternoon, we see the pups tumbling around and exploring their territory. A deer wanders into the yard, nibbling the flowers Roxanne tries valiantly but vainly to nurture. Charlie and Maggie, Joe and Rox's border collie and therefore Charlie's "cousin" (in my lexicon, relatives' dogs are all Charlie's cousins), are excited at the opportunity to chase the deer away. It's all a game to them until someone—namely Charlie—discovers deer droppings and, in order to share them with me, promptly rolls in the smelly mess and proudly presents himself.

"Great, Charlie! Now we'll have to find you a bath!" I wrinkle my nose in distaste.

Rox and I resolve this stinky problem by taking the dogs for a long walk. They wade in and out of the irrigation ditches, Maggie chasing her ball obsessively. Charlie ignores the ball and focuses on the many strange and wonderful smells to investigate. He loves water enough that he manages to wash away all the mess he rolled in.

🌲🌼🌲

On Sunday morning we borrow Joe's pickup and drive to the Mission in St. Ignatius. Mass features native language and music with drumming. The congregation is almost completely Native American and appears to be a close-knit community, but the parishioners nod and smile in a friendly way that makes us feel welcome.

The curving walls and ceilings of this small church are beautifully decorated by 58 murals and frescos painted by Brother Carignano, a cook at the mission when the chapel was built between 1891 and 1893. They depict St. Ignatius of Loyola, founder of the Society of Jesus (the Jesuits) for whom the mission and town were named, scenes from the Old and New Testaments and pictures of other early Jesuits and saints. The beauty of Brother Carignano's work is particularly impressive since this Italian brother had no formal artistic training.

The mission was founded by Jesuit Fr. Peter DeSmet and has been an important center for the Flathead, Kootenai, Pend'Oreille and other tribes in this region. Joe works as an attorney for the tribes, representing the members' environmental interests.

When we get back to Joe's, I'm ready for a nap. Late last night Charlie woke us barking ferociously at some wild creature, probably a fox or coyote. Or perhaps the deer had snuck back under cover of darkness to attack the roses again.

After my nap I spend time with my maps and guidebooks to figure out our next destination. The Mo is not equipped with a GPS system, but I enjoy looking at maps to get a more-encompassing view of where I'm going so I can plan the route before I get behind the wheel. Maybe I just prefer being in control of my destination rather than leaving it to a computer without a heart.

Montana is huge and very beautiful. In *Travels with Charley,* John Steinbeck wrote about his "love affair" with Montana; the parts I've seen on previous visits explain why he loved this state. We'll likely visit parts of Wyoming and Idaho before returning to Washington.

On Monday, we join Joe's family and watch the Memorial Day parade through the streets of Polson. As dusk falls on our last night here, I take Charlie for a walk across the fields, knee-high with wet grass following the rain. A pheasant rooster squawks a couple times and a flock of geese call to each other off in the distance. Lupine and delphinium add bright blue spots among the grasses and the many unfamiliar wildflowers.

Tuesday morning we head north following the Flathead River, a wild green torrent over its banks in some places. The mountains are magnificent but the road construction is awful—we're driving along at

60 miles an hour and suddenly, without warning, the pavement disappears and we're on sand and gravel. I manage, barely, to get the Mo slowed.

I'm excited to see my first pronghorn antelope on the rolling, bare land south of Browning. There isn't much else to see on this stretch.

We spend a night in Choteau known for its rich dinosaur digs. Charlie would have liked a giant bone to gnaw on, but dinosaurs have never held great interest for me. Choteau, known as the front porch of the Rocky Mountains, has baseball and softball fields, a rodeo grounds and not much else, though Charlie meets his first prairie dogs here. They sit at the top of their holes, whistling and chirping to get his attention. When he gives chase they dive below to safety, undoubtedly holding their sides and laughing uproariously.

I haven't made reservations for our next destination, Great Falls. As we are looking for the visitor's center to get recommendations for an RV park, we approach a railroad trestle with a sign warning that overhead clearance is 13 feet. I'm not sure of the Mo's height but it's pretty tall. I wince, grit my teeth and drive under, hoping not to hear any sickening scraping or crunching. I am relieved to get through without any incident and later discover—right there on my windshield—a notice that says the Mo is 12 feet high.

While in Great Falls we visit the Charlie Russell Museum and spend several hours viewing his paintings, sculptures and drawings. We also visit Giant Springs, an upwelling of underground water coming from limestone mountains many miles away. It is part of the series of falls and rapids that forced Lewis and Clark to portage 18 miles. We explore a Western store where I find a pair of cowboy boots on sale and a pair of nice buckskin work gloves.

Heading south to Jackson Hole, Wyoming, I know I need to be alone. I write in my blog: "It is hard trying to be a hostess and still do what I need to do. For short stints it might be fun to have friends along, but not for the long haul. I have work to do—even though I am not entirely sure what it is."

While Marian keeps Charlie occupied with constant petting as I drive, I reflect on the many friends who are thinking about me and praying for me. I trust that my journey will direct me to where I am supposed to be. All I can do is listen and discern where God is leading me. I know from experience that even if I don't listen very well, God will figure out a way to get me to where I am supposed to be. God knows I am trying, and that counts for a lot.

As we drive over these vast miles, Marian and I talk about John's accident, what she saw, what she remembers. We make peace with the misunderstandings that resulted.

"So, I'm really curious, Marian, why did you tell the insurance company what you did? About the accident?"

"I was just frightened, Maureen," she says as she rubs Charlie's ear. "I don't know why, or what I thought would happen if we sued the insurance company. I just was afraid."

"I understand." And I do. Her parents lost their North Dakota farm in the Depression. She doesn't trust banks or courts to be fair. She is part of that self-reliant generation.

We drive across mountains and plains, crossing the Continental Divide twice. Eight hours later we arrive in the Teton Valley, near the Idaho/Wyoming border. I've never been in this part of Idaho and find the Tetons amazing. High rocky peaks stand out like sharp fists defying travelers to attempt them. I imagine how intimidated the first settlers must have been to see them.

The road into Jackson Hole through the mountains is steep and winding. We climb up 10 percent grades through Teton Pass (8,431 feet elevation), our ears popping. Then we roll back down 10 percent grades into Jackson. Coming down that steep run makes the brakes smoke, even though I use the exhaust brake and use second gear most of the way. Some of the curves are 25 mph or less. Later a truck driver warns me to let the brakes cool off before tackling slopes like this.

Charlie has a harrowing morning in Jackson encountering some monstrous creatures. He meets a huge black Great Dane, which fortunately turns out to be friendly. Then he meets an even larger buffalo, which fortunately turns out to be stuffed. He sniffs at it repeatedly, seeming unsure what to do, then starts growling. I move him along before he makes a scene. Several tourists are watching the encounter and smile in amusement.

Charlie has discovered his new favorite place from which to view the world. He is able to jump up on the dashboard of the Mo, which is wide enough for him to sit or lie on. He looks very cute and kind of regal lying up there and earns a new nickname: Dashboard Dog.

Undoubtedly people walking by chuckle at a big golden retriever standing on the dash looking out the window. John Steinbeck was right, even if his Charley was a standard poodle. Dogs are amazing ambassadors and conversation starters. I can't imagine a better diplomat than a handsome golden retriever with a happy grin.

Leaving Jackson we head south following the Snake River. We are admiring mountains in every direction: the Gros Ventres, Wyoming and Salt River ranges on the east, the Caribou range west of us and the Webster Range southwest. The lilacs are still blooming here in early June, a good month behind Portland. They are even behind Polson, where the lilacs were just finishing up when we left a week ago. The winters here must be long and harsh.

We've met interesting people on this trip. In Great Falls I spoke with a man from North Carolina who was working for his site rental at the RV park. He and his wife each worked 16 hours a week collecting garbage, cleaning restrooms and other chores. I met a couple from Florida who were headed to Alaska. Two women from Holland who rented an RV to visit Yellowstone and Glacier National Parks occupied another site in the RV park. At the Russell Museum we talked with a couple from the Channel Islands in Great Britain.

After wending our way across Idaho, stopping overnight near Mountain Home, we arrive back in Oregon. Mike meets us on I-84 at Biggs to take Marian back home. We unload her things, and she and Mike head north. Alone again, I head west towards Portland.

I will spend the next few days in Portland celebrating the wedding of a friend, attending my final meeting of the parish Pastoral Council, and cantoring for the Sunday evening contemplative Mass. I have treasured participating in this beautiful, quiet, prayerful liturgy. Giving up singing at this Mass is one of the more difficult sacrifices I am making to pursue my travel and soul-searching.

I continue to have misgivings and second thoughts about the enormity of the changes I've made in my life. My ongoing questioning of this decision to travel is becoming like a pesky next-door neighbor: taking up a lot of my time but not really helping in any way. I know I have to keep going forward, at least for the time being, and give it enough time. I pray the fruits of this effort will be worthwhile.

Chapter 4
Trekking On

We are all pilgrims on the wearisome road
Of our life, every end becomes a beginning.
There is no resting place, no abiding city.
Every answer becomes a new question;
Every good fortune a new beginning.
Ours is to trek on.
~ Karl Rahner, SJ

"In the Jewish tradition, when there is a wedding in which one of the parents has passed away, God goes to the Garden of Eden to get the soul of that parent and take them to the wedding so they can share in the joy of their child," Fr. Peter Byrne is telling my newly married young friend Sarah, her husband Kelly, and their family and friends.

Sarah's father passed away when she was 12. I reflect on Kristin's and Karl's weddings and think how comforting Fr. Peter's words might have been for them. Both of my kids were married without their dad's presence. Kristin's husband, Ryan, had lost both his parents to cancer by the age of 12. Just two months ago Karl and Dee had hurriedly exchanged vows at the Courthouse in Vancouver so her father, who was dying of cancer, could be present. He died within weeks of their marriage.

Fr. Peter talks about the joy of growing old together and being there for each other, especially at the time of death. "It is the last gift we can give to our beloved spouse: to help them transition to the Next Life."

This breaks my heart. Not being with John when he died to reassure and comfort him was incredibly painful. We had been together so long; why didn't I get to be with him on his last day?

I shed copious tears during this wedding; they are probably tears that had been held back for too long and are healing. Unfortunately, this also means my eye makeup is a mess, and I have a date after the wedding, my first in almost two years.

☀ ✿ ☀

I had not found a man I was interested in since Lance had ended our relationship, despite my hopes that I could some day find another man to share my life. Ironically, in the weeks I have been preparing to leave Oregon for an extended period of time, two new relationship possibilities surfaced.

The first was Keith. His sister, my dear friend Cate, told Keith of my blog, and he had been reading it. At one point he made a comment, and we exchanged email addresses and began to correspond. As we wrote back and forth, a friendship blossomed that seemed promising.

I was intrigued by the sweet, flirtatious nature that emerged from his messages and wanted to meet him in person. I am planning to spend time in Yakima the weekend before the 4th of July. John's extended family always celebrates with a picnic, providing an opportunity to see everyone before I take off next month. I'm unsure how long I'll be gone, and I want to tell family goodbye before I leave.

I sent Keith an email suggesting that after my visit to Yakima I might drive over to Tacoma to visit him.

"Well, I would like to meet you," he wrote back, "but I've been seeing someone, and I don't think she'd like it very much if I spent time hanging out with you. So probably not the best idea."

"Oh. Well, never mind, then," I responded, a little irritated he had been carrying on a very friendly email conversation with me when he wasn't available.

"Well, yeah. Sorry. But I look forward to continuing to read your blog posts."

Whatever, I thought to myself, crossing Keith mentally off my list of prospects. Not available and obviously a little flakey.

A couple weeks before this exchange, a friend had introduced me to Troy. He had wanted to learn more about my travel plans. I'm setting off to join him for a movie as I leave Sarah's wedding reception. He has suggested meeting at a theater very convenient for him but not at all convenient for me; we end up not seeing the movie I wanted to see, and he has forgotten he had a dinner engagement with friends, so our date is cut short.

Sunday morning Troy calls me.

"Man, I can't believe I double-booked last night. I don't know how I forgot I had that dinner scheduled. Guess I was just so happy you followed up with me it slipped my mind. Why don't you let me make it up to you? What are you doing Monday?"

"Well, what did you have in mind? I have to clear a few things out of the house in the morning now that it's sold." I had left some furniture in the house to make it look occupied while it was on the market. My brother Michael was driving down to get it for his home. "But I'm free that afternoon."

"I was thinking we should take a drive up the Columbia River Gorge, go explore the fruit stands in Hood River, maybe find some fresh cherries, stop for lunch along the river somewhere. Just get to know each other a little better."

"That sounds nice. When were you thinking about leaving?"

"I have a meeting at 9 not too far from your house; maybe I could meet you there around 10:30 or 11."

"I think 11 would work. I'll see you Monday morning."

🌲🌼🌲

After working for so many years, I am delighted to be off messing around on a Monday and to have a partner in crime. Since retiring I have become convinced that the best weather of the week is on Monday, and this day is no exception. It's warm without being too hot; the often-gusty Gorge is calm, the river shimmers in the sun like glass, reflecting the blue sky.

Our conversation ranges from deep philosophical/spiritual issues to practical backgrounds, future hopes and dreams. He was a finance executive with a Northwest company; his job ended when that company was bought by a national corporation.

We have a lot in common. He lost his wife six years ago to cancer. We are both Catholics and trying to discover how God is calling us to use our gifts to help others.

"I'm working on starting a non-profit to help women who are victims of domestic violence get their lives back together," he explains as we sit in the sun at a park in Cascade Locks sharing a bottle of pinot gris we found at one of the fruit stands. "I think I can help them get their finances sorted out, maybe help them define their career goals and find jobs to support themselves and their kids."

"Wow, that sounds like a great goal! I'm hoping my travels can inspire me to find something I can give my passion and energy to. I'd like to find a mission I can believe in that will help me make a difference."

Troy is friendly, positive and seems pretty happy-go-lucky with a goofy sense of humor, but he can also be focused, decisive and in charge. He seems like the kind of man people would turn to when they need help or advice. In fact, he tells me he is helping his younger brother sue a large hotel chain after an injury left him wheelchair-bound and describes his recent visit to New Orleans to help friends whose son had committed suicide.

He seems to have many good friends, both men and women, and enjoys fishing with his buddies. He describes himself as a Labrador retriever, which seems to fit.

We don't agree on everything but have some free-flowing, deep conversations for two people who have only met a couple times.

"This has been great," he says as he drops me off at the house to pick up my car, which I've borrowed back from Karl to run errands while I'm in town. "It's so nice to just take a relaxing day to talk and enjoy ourselves."

"Yeah, it has. Our society has such a need to be productive, to always be doing something. We hardly ever take the time to sit back and look at the beauty around us and give thanks for that. Or just spend time getting to know each other as people. But sometimes I think it's that down time that really matters.

"If we're always so busy taking care of stuff out there, we never take the time to take care of stuff inside, and that is some of the most intimidating, scary but important work we can ever do. Because until we take the time to find our true selves, how can we possibly figure out what God wants for us?"

"Wow, pretty and a philosopher, too." Troy kisses me goodbye.

We undoubtedly will see more of each other before I leave the Northwest.

Tuesday I sign the papers selling the house, which should close on Friday, and then pick up the Saturn I have purchased. Gary shows me how to hook up and then unhook the car. It's challenging, but I am confident I can handle it.

I'm waiting to attend another friend's wedding in mid-July before I head east. Since I will not be visiting Keith in Tacoma, I call my older sister Colleen in Northern California.

"Hey, what are you doing the week after the 4th? Can you get some time off and come with me to Yosemite National Park? I've never been and always wanted to see it."

"Well, I have Mondays off so I could leave here on Friday if that works, and I can take a couple extra days off to go with you."

"Cool! I'll see you next Friday, the 6th, then."

Troy and I spend more time together before I leave for Yakima. He invites me to stop on my way to California and spend a couple days in Central Oregon with him as he visits friends. I'll be driving down from

Yakima on Highway 97, which travels through Central Oregon, so it will work out well.

Taking another shakedown trip turns out to be a good decision before I head across the country.

Leaving Yakima Monday morning I am driving south into Central Oregon when I notice my low-coolant warning light has come on. I pull over to check and the coolant reservoir is quite low. Personally, I am impressed that I am able to find the coolant reservoir; of course, it helps that it is labeled.

There are very few towns along this route to buy coolant or find a mechanic. I manage to get to Madras where I buy additional coolant to add, but the diesel mechanic is too busy to help me figure out why my coolant is leaking. In Bend, Troy and his friend check it and can't find any problems.

After enjoying two days in Bend with Troy and his friends, I head south Thursday. I make it to the Mount Shasta area of Northern California before the low coolant light comes on again. There is no place to stop or find help until Weed where I buy two more gallons of coolant and refill the reservoir. The rig continues to leak coolant, but it is not gushing out so, although I am uncomfortable, I keep going. Besides, I don't know what else to do.

The farther south I drive, the hotter the weather gets. It is hard to keep the Mo cool, and Charlie is panting heavily. When I stop in Corning and pull into an RV park for the night, the heat is suffocating—114°. After parking and hooking up to electric and water, I turn on both air conditioners, take a quick dip in the swimming pool and then hose Charlie down.

Because I am only staying for the night and the site is long enough, I leave the car hooked to the Mo, filling the entire space. The next morning I stop at a shopping center for groceries and more coolant. As I park, I hear someone yelling.

"Hey, hey you!" And then something unintelligible. I look around. A large man with long hair and tattoos is standing in the parking lot yelling and waving his arms to get my attention. This is unnerving, but I open my driver's window a few inches to hear him.

"Hey, there's somethin' wrong with your car. It looks like it came loose," he says, introducing himself as Bill.

I get out to check and, indeed, the tow bar is loose. The cotter pin that locks the tow bar to the car is missing on one side. I don't know if someone intentionally removed the pin or if it worked loose, but it's a tight fit so that seems unlikely.

Bill recruits another man and the three of us try to put it back together. We can't make it fit, even after I unhook the car from the Mo. Bill discovers the tow bar was bent when the car came loose.

Corning is small but my helpers think the muffler shop a couple blocks beyond the RV park might be able to straighten it. Bill is helping his grandmother shop for groceries and offers to give me a ride to the muffler shop when they are finished.

"That's very kind of you," I tell him. "But if it's that close, I'll just walk over there. Thanks so much for your help; it would have been awful if I'd headed out with my car loose. It could have been disastrous." I offer him a $5 bill, which is all the cash I have, in thanks for his time and help.

"Nah," he says, waving it off. "Just say thanks to the Man Upstairs."

"I already have," I tell him gratefully.

I walk towards the muffler shop carrying the bar with me. The temperature is already scorching, and I soon regret walking. Undoubtedly the heat makes me more sympathetic or at least pathetic. Tim, who owns the muffler shop, tells me he can't straighten the bar with his equipment.

"But I need to go to NAPA shortly and they've got machinists who can probably fix it," he says. "As soon as my mom gets here to cover the office we can go over there." Charlie and I practically empty his water cooler while we wait. Charlie, who has gamely walked with me but is on the verge of overheating in his heavy coat, remains at the shop with Tim's mother while we try to find help for the tow bar.

Unfortunately, no one is available at NAPA to straighten the bar today. Tim promises to find someone to straighten it, so I leave the Saturn with him until my return trip next week, and Charlie and I hit the road, hours behind schedule.

🌲🕸🌲

I meet Colleen in Potter Valley, and she follows me in her car so we can more easily explore Yosemite.

Our first destination is a campground north of Cloverdale on the Russian River, and it's 10:30 when we finally arrive. I back into the one remaining site, feeling thankful I don't have to unhook a car. I connect the water and electricity in the dark, making a mental note to add a flashlight to my tools.

The next morning we stop for fuel before leaving Cloverdale. My low coolant light has come on again. With all the excitement of my car coming loose, I had put that out of my mind. The reservoir is almost empty again, and coolant is running out of the engine like someone forgot to turn off a faucet.

I pay for the diesel but am told the station doesn't carry RV coolant, though a nearby auto parts store will likely have it. I bend down and look under the Mo trying to figure out why the coolant is leaking.

"Whoa, what's happening?" a man in a dirty Grateful Dead t-shirt and ragged jeans asks as he ambles over. "Lemme see what I can find," he offers after I explain that my motor home is losing coolant. He bends down, weaving a little, and pokes around.

"Lookee here," he says, pointing. "Here's your problem; you got a hole in this hose."

Indeed, a pinprick hole in the radiator hose is spraying coolant. Realizing I'll have to figure out a way to patch that at least temporarily, I thank him and drive down the block to the auto parts store. Auto parts stores are outside my comfort zone; in the last few days I've been in far too many of them for my taste.

I explain the situation to the man at the parts counter, and he comes out to investigate how to patch my leaky hose. As we are looking at the engine, a young man walks up and watches us.

"Wow, I guess men really are fascinated by big engines," I say to him, smiling.

"I'm a diesel mechanic and thought maybe I could help in some way," he says.

"Thank you, God!" I whisper and then turn and greet him with an even bigger smile.

"Yeah, we're trying to patch this because it seems to be leaking pretty seriously," I say. "I'd love whatever help you can give me."

"Well, I'm not sure I've got my tools in my truck; let me check, and if I do, I'll see if I can help. My name's Matt," he says, extending his hand. I grasp it like it's a life preserver.

"Matt, I'm Maureen, and I am so glad to meet you!"

Matt gets his tools, which by a great stroke of luck are in his pickup. He dons his coveralls in the already intense heat and begins exploring the damage.

"You know, a patch isn't going to help this," he says scooting out from under the Mo after a few minutes. "Look, this hose is shot." He sticks his finger into the rubber hose, and it appears to be made from porous fabric; coolant sprays out every time he touches it.

Back into the parts store I go to find a hose that fits.

Matt crawls under the Mo to drain the entire engine, a very messy job, and begins removing the hose.

"So, Matt," I squat down to watch as he is working, "has anyone ever told you're the answer to a prayer?"

He laughs. "No, but I have been told I seem to think I'm God."

"Well, you're without a doubt a gift from God, and you can tell that to any young lady you're trying to impress," I stand back up.

"Can we get that on videotape?" he responds, laughing as he resurfaces from under the Mo to get the replacement hose I found.

At this point a guy in a "mobile mechanic" van drives up. Apparently someone at the auto parts store had called him.

"Hey, you got a license to do that?" he demands of Matt.

"I don't need a license to help a friend," Matt shoots back. More quietly he mutters, "I might not have a license, but at least I have all my teeth."

The man, unkempt and grizzled, continues to badger Matt, demanding he be given the job he was called to do.

"Hey, I didn't call you." I step towards him as he sits in the van. "I didn't ask you to come here. I don't know who did. Thank you for stopping but, as you can see, I have someone helping me, we have it covered, and your help isn't needed here today."

Angrily he threatens to call Matt's boss and tell him Matt is taking jobs away from people who have a right to them. Seeing that he isn't going to convince Matt to leave, he eventually drives away.

Colleen and I take Charlie for a short walk and then do some grocery shopping at the adjacent Safeway during the two hours Matt is working on the Mo. His cousins, who were at the recycling center next door turning in pop bottles and cans, join Colleen and me as we watch Matt finish the work and clean up spilled coolant.

"I brought them over here yesterday," Matt waves towards the recycling center, "but the place was closed. That's the reason we're here today."

I utter another prayer of thanks. It seems amazing that a diesel mechanic just happens to show up at the exact moment I need one. Someone is clearly taking care of me.

Matt tells me he had just turned 29, making him barely a year older than my daughter. I wish him a belated happy birthday. I can't really wish enough good things for this Good Samaritan.

As he finishes up I offer to pay him for his time and ask him how much would be fair. I feel certain he did this to help, not with the idea of getting paid. I have no idea how much diesel mechanics earn.

His cousins made $38 recycling cans. "You got $38.50?" he smiles.

I feel he deserves much more but I hand him two $20s.

"Really, you have been such a wonderful help. Can't I give you more?" I offer.

He refuses.

"Well, at least take this as a late birthday present." I hand him a $25 restaurant gift card. This young man spent more than two hours of his Saturday fixing my motor home and all he wants is to match what his cousins made from their recycling.

As we are finishing up, the Toothless Mobile Mechanic returns, again trying to pick a fight.

"Hey, I'm gonna call your boss and tell him you're taking work away from other people," he threatens, getting out of his van. "You ain't got no right to be takin' food outta my mouth."

I think to myself: more like beer out of your mouth, mister. He smells as though he's already been drowning his sorrows.

Matt tells him to get lost and takes a step toward him.

"Yeah, go ahead. Hit me. Go right ahead. I'll get your ass fired," says the old man. "You'll end up in jail."

I step in between them and push Matt towards his truck.

"Just go, Matt. This guy's a bully who isn't worth wasting your time on. Let it go. Please, just drive away. C'mon guys, get him out of here," I implore his cousins to get him into his truck.

Then I turn on Toothless.

"You have no business being here, harassing me and him. I did not call and ask for your help, and I can't help it if someone else did. You have no right to demand anything from me or threaten this young man. He's been kind and generous to help me, and he doesn't deserve your threats and bullying. Now just go away and leave him alone. Now! G'wan! Get!" I stamp my foot and yell at him like I would address a dog barking threateningly at Charlie and me.

Finally Matt's cousins push and pull him into the truck and they leave. Toothless also gives up and leaves, still grumbling. Later I call the auto parts store and tell them about his behavior. "I don't think you should use him in the future," I suggest.

Cloverdale has yielded an angel and an antagonist, I think, as we drive southeast towards Yosemite.

Chapter 5
Seeing with New Eyes

*The real voyage of discovery consists not
in seeking new landscapes, but in having
new eyes.*

~ Marcel Proust

This part of California is new to me. The landscape between the Sacramento River Delta and the High Sierra country is rolling hills covered in golden brown grass and liberally sprinkled with deep-green-leafed oak trees. I imagine how striking the country looks in the fall when the oak leaves turn bright gold, or in spring when the grasses are pale green. This country feels solid and admirable and peaceful in the height of summer.

The road up to Yosemite is steep and tightly curved. I worry about driving the Mo back down and hope to find a better route.

We spend our days exploring the Yosemite Valley, stopping often to take pictures. The granite rock formations of El Capitan, Half Dome and around Yosemite Falls are breathtaking. The rock is less jagged than the mountains in Montana and Wyoming, but no less imposing. The tall, straight Ponderosa pines add additional beauty.

We drive Colleen's Camry over Tioga Pass. The beauty is awe-inspiring but the altitude is what truly takes our breath away as we drive to an elevation of nearly 10,000 feet. It is the highest motor vehicle pass in California, possibly one of the highest in the country.

We circle back across Sonora Pass, a narrow and winding road with 25 percent grades. It's a slightly lower elevation but the steep grades and hairpin turns are more challenging. Signs clearly advise against trying this route with RVs, trucks and trailers. Of course there's always got to be one smart guy who thinks he's such an outstanding driver he can ignore the warnings. We pass him stuck in a ditch with a steep drop-off a couple feet beyond his travel trailer.

Colleen and I share stories about growing up together with a mother who seemed incapable of approval or even love for her oldest children.

"Oh my gosh," Colleen says one night as we sit around the campfire sipping wine. "I remember when I was absolutely devastated, just sure that I had leprosy. I had this spot on my arm that wouldn't go away. I was sobbing; I just knew my skin was going to start falling off, and I was going to die. Mom was working or at a meeting or something that night, and when she came home I was so upset. I got out of bed to tell her. She just looked at me and said, 'Oh for Heaven's sake. That's nothing. Get back to bed!' "

"I remember the year I had several A's on my report card and Mom wanted to know why I'd gotten a C in deportment. Nothing positive about the A's, just criticism for the C." I shake my head.

"I think she'd have been ecstatic if I ever got an A," Colleen shrugs. "But then, you were always her favorite."

"Oh, not hardly. You were the first-born. I was the second girl just 15 months later. I think Mom and Dad were shell-shocked by then. And then Michael came and they had their boy. He was their favorite."

"No, Thomas and Shirley were their favorites," Colleen says with a sigh. I nod.

After a few minutes of silence, Colleen continues.

"I butted heads with her so many times over so many things till finally I just gave up, realizing I was never going to please her.

"Like in high school when everyone was wearing skirts above the knee, and I tried to tell her that, she just insisted mine had to cover my knees. And then you, you just rolled your skirt up after you left the house in the morning."

I laugh at the memory. "Well, I didn't want to make her angry, and I knew I'd never win that argument. I just kept trying to stay on her good side, do things well, the way she expected, hoping some day she'd be proud of me or tell me she loved me or something. I just couldn't give up. But part of me still wanted to be myself, or at least not look like a dork. I know you got to a place where you just didn't care any more. Sometimes I wish I could have."

"Well, you're a Leo. You think everyone should love you."

"Yeah. What's wrong with that?" I smile and get up to refill our wine glasses. We sit awhile longer enjoying the stars and quiet, sharing memories.

"But what really ticked me off about you," Colleen says as we settle in for the night, "is how you always borrowed my clothes without asking and then threw them on the floor of the closet or under your bed."

"Oh bull! I never!" I head off to my bed, grinning. Every time we talk about our growing up years this story surfaces, and I have absolutely no recollection of such atrocities.

With our parents gone now, Colleen is the only person I've known all my life. I'm thankful we've had this time to share and nurture our friendship.

But as I lie in bed, sleep refuses to come. My mind is busy digesting our conversation. Much as I hate to admit it, Colleen is right: I do want everyone to love me, though deep down I wonder if I am lovable at all.

My sense of unworthiness has been like a second shadow from my earliest memories. One of the most common phrases to come out of my mouth is "I'm sorry." I hate to disappoint people or have them upset with me. Does this stem from feeling from my very beginnings that I was an intrusion, an inconvenience?

Colleen was only six months old when Mom became pregnant with me. My parents were just starting out, had been married barely two years and were struggling financially. Dad left college a few credits short of completing his degree in entomology to support his new family. They lived in a strange city, far from family and friends. Undoubtedly I was unplanned, an accident.

Was my mother dismayed or angry to find out she was pregnant again so soon after Colleen had been born? Did she cry when she found out, or yell in fury, also part of her nature? Did she feel overwhelmed? Did Dad feel burdened and a little frightened of the responsibilities he'd taken on?

Were my parents disappointed I wasn't a son? Three years later Michael arrived, followed in the next ten years by Dennis, Thomas and then Shirley. I was the scrawny little sandwich filling between the first child and the first son.

Something convinced me I was an inconvenience, a mistake, unwanted. A persistent, nasty voice whispered to me I had no right to be born and had to make up for that by being as perfect and unobtrusive as possible, by fitting in without making a peep. And yet that is not who I really am. I want a place at the table. I want to feel I belong, am valued and appreciated. Being a Leo, I thrive on recognition. Feeling unappreciated or unseen is my version of hell.

Years ago when I became a mother, Mom and I talked about the inadequate praise she gave us.

"It just felt like we could never measure up to your expectations," I said, holding a squirming three-year-old Karl on my lap. "Like nothing I did was enough to win your love."

"I always thought if I praised you kids too much, you'd get swelled heads and not try to do better. I only ever wanted the best for you. I guess I didn't understand that praise, support and unconditional love are the best ways to raise happy, successful children. I'm sorry I didn't give you what you needed. But I hope you know I always loved you, every one of you." Her eyes filled with tears.

As an adult now I accept that. Children don't understand when their mother comes home exhausted or frustrated. Maybe someone had treated Mom rudely and she was feeling that rejection the night she cavalierly dismissed Colleen's hysteria about leprosy. But a wounded child deep inside me still needs reassurance that I am lovable.

I grew up wearing hand-me-downs from my sister, neighbors, friends and people I didn't know. I usually had holes in the soles of my shoes before the school year ended. In the winter we often had to stretch a pot of pinto beans over several days to feed the family. Birthday parties, vacations and even television were luxuries we couldn't afford. I often felt I didn't fit in with most of my classmates.

Putting all these ingredients together, I grew up convinced I was inadequate. I had little self-confidence or self-esteem. I was shy, afraid of saying or doing the wrong thing. I was also a tom-boy, perhaps sensing my father might appreciate me more if I played sports well, went fishing with him, was handy and capable and competent and not a silly girl afraid to get my hands dirty. Sadly, though I was the best tree-climber and fastest runner in the neighborhood, mechanical skills eluded me.

In spite of my insecurities, I have always held deep within my core a conviction that I am a good and lovable person who deserves to be noticed, to live and contribute and be accepted and acknowledged. Is this my soul, reminding me that God loves me unconditionally, that I, as a human being, am inherently good and worthy of love? Perhaps it is God-within-me, the spark of Divine we all have as part of creation. Life coach Martha Beck, in her book, *Steering by Starlight*, calls this force the Stargazer, that part of us that never loses sight of our true destiny and continually reminds us of our greater purpose, beyond fears and insecurities.

Ultimately this is one purpose of my journey: to test myself and find the peace and silence that will allow me to listen to my Stargazer, my soul, my God. I hope this also helps me love myself better, be kind to myself and let go of those old painful messages that suggest I have little worth and value.

🔺🌼🔺

On our last day at Yosemite we take Charlie for a long walk, and he splashes in the creek that flows through the campground. Someone had dammed up a little area leaving a fairly deep pool. Charlie steps into it, can't touch bottom and has to swim briefly. He seems a little frantic. His panic reminds me of the insecurities we all face: not knowing where the bottom is (or where we'll sleep tomorrow night or if we'll ever be happy, or the multiple things we worry about). He has no problem swimming—he won't drown if he can't touch bottom. It's just frightening to lose control, the surprise of having the ground suddenly disappear below his feet. I understand.

The big scary hill coming down from the Sierras is, indeed, big and scary; but according to everyone I asked, it is the best way out of Yosemite. I keep the Mo in second gear, keep the exhaust brake on and the speed down to around 20-25. It is early morning, there is limited traffic, and I encounter no problems, not even smoking brakes.

I know this time of waiting, listening and praying is important work right now. Being with others distracts from my interior journey. But it is also important to make peace with loved ones. As I share, experience and listen, I grow, stretch, and learn more about myself. I'm unsure what the coming weeks hold, but though I can't touch bottom, I trust I can swim well enough to be safe.

After parting with Colleen near Sacramento, I arrive back in Corning around 3 to pick up the Saturn and pay my whopping $35 bill. What could have been dual disasters have cost me less than $100 because of the kindness of strangers.

🌲🌼🌲

The California Coast between Eureka and Crescent City where I spend two nights on the way back to Oregon is covered with pebbles, not sand. At first glance the pebbles are unimpressive. But on closer inspection, each is a magical little gem—agates, quartz, jasper, granite—polished by the ocean, sand and other rocks. Walking with Charlie, I find intriguing rocks to inspect and sometimes put in my pocket. I end up with a selection of rocks from Stone Lagoon beach.

The rocks bring to mind my dad, a rockhound. He loved beauty—especially in nature—but was too busy trying to feed six kids to explore his creative side: art and music.

Rocks are so common and easy to overlook. My sister-in-law Brenda likes to look for heart-shaped rocks on the beach. I think of her and, watching carefully, I bend over and pick up a rock with a rough heart shape. I see that the rounded top has been broken, probably forced into a harder rock by waves. Having this little piece broken off creates the heart shape. What was once rounded and intact has become a little more interesting and desirable because of its brokenness. I think being broken can make us whole, can create new hearts in us.

I pick up a rock that is sparkling quartz on one side, the other side plain gray rock. If the plain side had been facing up, I wouldn't have noticed it. I wonder how many rocks we pass over because their beautiful side is hidden. How many people do we pass over because the side that is visible is unattractive or dull?

We must keep turning rocks over, searching for the beautiful sides. We forget how abundant beauty and goodness are when we dwell on the things that are wrong with our country and our world.

I used to be reluctant to discuss my faith with others. But on this journey I make it a point to give God credit, to talk about why I am doing this, to be open, kind and forgiving. The incident from the previous week haunts me some. Could I have handled Toothless differently? Instead of responding with anger, I could have tried to understand him. He was missing out on a job, even though I hadn't called him or asked the shop to call him. Maybe he needed that money to pay his rent. My negative reaction to him didn't feel authentic but cynical, the sign of a tired heart that has forgotten how to be a child and accept things at face value without judging them or looking through negative filters. Maybe I missed his beautiful side.

Driving back to Oregon, I think about my roots and my home. I was born in Idaho and grew up in Yakima, my dad's hometown. The year I turned 28, John and I moved to Oregon, which has become home. Kristin and Karl were born here; most of my friends are here.

Declaring my state of residency is perplexing. Full-time RVers often declare residency in Texas, South Dakota or Florida for tax purposes. I need to re-license the Saturn so this is something I must decide soon. In spite of possible tax benefits of changing residency, I feel connected to Oregon. Nearly all my networking contacts are in the Portland area should I choose to return to work at some point.

Troy meets me at my next stop in Florence on the central Oregon Coast, an hour north of Coos Bay. We drive down to see Kristin and Ryan, who seem a little overwhelmed by Troy. He is a large man, tall and solidly built, with a voice to match. He is enthusiastic and positive, laughs often, and is something of a good ol' boy, a hail-fellow-well-met. He's also very intelligent, astute and confident—sometimes bordering on being full of himself.

For the first couple of weeks we were dating I thought Troy might be the answer to my prayers. Assuming God's hand is in things when it really isn't can take me off on wrong roads and get me lost quicker than fog on the Oregon Coast.

I know I will never find a perfect partner, but after spending several days with Troy, I find some things about him are becoming a little irritating. Not everything in life is certain or static; some things are mystery, in flux, paradoxes. He is action-oriented and sometimes action is not the right answer. He seems fairly conservative politically though doesn't appear interested in politics, and his spirituality feels more conservative than mine. Sometimes he seems to imply that he knows the way and I'm a little mixed up. It feels occasionally like he is trying to lead me down the right paths. I think we all have different paths, and we need to let God work in everyone as God chooses.

It seems to me that many religious people try to control God by fitting their faith into little man-made boxes. By following "the rules," obeying the dictates, following dogma, observing traditions, doing what the Church tells them, and having "correct" beliefs, they feel they are in control of God. But I believe we cannot control God by how we see or think or believe. God doesn't fit into boxes.

It is arrogant to insist that one's beliefs are best or that other ways of believing are inferior. Like the Pharisees who often tested Jesus, judging others based on our own spiritual experiences is a way of putting ourselves above God, of setting ourselves on altars to be admired.

Instead of being full of ourselves because we read the Bible regularly or go to church every Sunday, we need to empty ourselves and make room for God, to let God enter our open hearts, our open minds and accept God as God comes to us.

🌲🦋🌲

As we spend a couple of days together on the Oregon Coast, I am feeling pressure from Troy to make a commitment to him before I leave or, more subtly, to abandon this trip altogether.

"I can't just have you out wandering around the country without any ties," he says one day. "What if you meet someone else? What if you decide not to come back?"

Well, I think to myself, *I guess that would mean I wasn't interested in coming back to you, wouldn't it? Duh!*

"So what size ring do you wear?" he continues. "I have a friend who can get any style and always has a great selection." Maybe it's his assuming he knows what's best for me that I find so irritating.

Out of curiosity I look at rings one day and have my ring finger measured (it's an 8, for the record). The idea of marrying, having someone special in my life to lean on, staying in Portland and abandoning my quest is appealing. But I am determined to follow this journey; it is something I must do. If this is the right relationship, it will wait for me to finish my work. It will happen in God's time, and it will become clear to me. I need to learn better how to discern God's presence, God's will in my life.

Earlier this month I met with Fr. Peter. He suggested perhaps God doesn't have a "specific" plan for us but wants us to come up with a plan ourselves and offer it to God. "Surprise me," God says. "See what you can come up with that will delight you and me."

I like this idea: figuring out what would make me happiest. But it means I have some serious soul-searching to do to discover my deep longing. What makes me want to get up each morning, what gives me life?

During my discussion with Fr. Peter, we talked about Troy and his possible role in my life. Fr. Peter reminded me of the work I had done to discern this current path for myself.

"This is something you feel called to do right now," he said. "You have to see it through. You need to take this time away. When you go, Troy needs to give you that time. He shouldn't contact you; he needs to just let you be alone, be with God. And you need to tell him that; make sure he respects your need for quiet, contemplative time."

I know he is right. I have made many sacrifices to get to this point, though it will be hard to insist Troy give me that space and freedom.

Troy returns to Portland and I remain in Florence, spending time with Kristin. She and Ryan have built a good life and seem content. They have a big garden. He brews outstanding beer, and she knits beautiful things. They go crabbing on the Bay and buy fresh fish off the docks. I have never wished anything for my children beyond that they be happy, satisfied with their life, have someone to love who loves them. And that God have a role there. I have always felt such a deep presence of God in my own life, despite frustrations and anger and questions. I am so thankful for the gift of faith passed on to me by my parents.

Mom was a convert to the Catholic faith, and her Protestant upbringing gave her a deep appreciation for scripture. She wasn't steeped in Catholic ritual and prayer as many cradle Catholics of the time were. The Rosary and other Marian devotions weren't as much a part of my life as the Bible, but her faith was deep and constant, and she passed her faith and love of God on to me. I feel blessed to have experienced my parents' devotion to God; it is the best inheritance they could have given me.

As I drive to Coos Bay to visit Kristin, I realize tomorrow, July 18, is my wedding anniversary. Those special dates get a bit easier every year. They are opportunities to remember the good times, the blessings we shared, the gifts of our children, our families, our friends, and our faith. This is the first anniversary since John died that I won't be living in the house we built together. Spending time with our children reminds me of the true home we built together: the family we raised.

While I have been blessed with beautiful weather much of my time on the coast, into each life some rain must fall, especially in Western Oregon. The morning of my wedding anniversary, I awake to rain. But everything brings its own blessing, and this rainy day gives me a good opportunity to reflect. I spend the day hibernating in the Mo, which has become my "womb," my safe and sacred space. It is my sanctuary while I wait for God and my new life.

One of the helpful guides I have found is the book *When the Heart Waits: Spiritual Direction for Life's Sacred Questions* by Sue Monk Kidd. Kidd writes about the "pilgrimage" of middle age that leads us to seek our true selves, to grow and become who God intended us to be. John of the Cross, Teresa of Avila, Thomas Merton, and other mystics wrote about this process: the contemplative journey of going into the depths of ourselves to find our true self.

Kidd writes that often in mid-life a sacred pull, perhaps from within our own hearts, draws us deeper into the mystery of ourselves and our relationship to God. This longing can plunge us into a maelstrom of feelings and questions and decisions.

Carl Jung claimed that "every midlife crisis is a spiritual crisis." He called this life phase the afternoon, a time for adapting to the inner world by developing the full and true self, a more real, more Christ-like self. He compared the transition from the morning to the afternoon phase to a difficult birth. The pain and struggle in my search feels a bit like labor. Perhaps I am straining to bring my inner self into the light, beginning to listen to voices I've avoided too long.

Kidd says in her book that waiting for God is like waiting for the birth of a child. This "gestation" time is critical for spiritual development and can't be hurried. This pilgrimage is my personal trip to Bethlehem, and I hope to birth a new, more authentic me. I have physically left behind my old self in many ways; I need to continue that process on a deeper level and replace that old self, that old life of masks, of being the person I think others expect me to be, with one that is true.

I think about the startling dream I had last night: In my dream I am walking and talking with a former neighbor and close friend for many years. As we walk, she points out my grave, barely discernible on the side of the path. No marker, just soil and rocks heaped up over it. I don't recall what she said to me, but I remember being startled that I had a grave because I didn't know I had died.

Perhaps the person I was when she and I were close friends is in the process of dying. But a new person is emerging from that death, one I hope will be more open, authentic and joyful.

I decide it's a good day to tackle my false selves. All of us learn to adjust our behavior and beliefs based on the expectations of important others. We fear the loss of love and approval if we do not meet these expectations, and so we develop ways of relating or reacting to life to protect ourselves from hurt. But the selves we develop to meet these expectations are often inauthentic; they do not represent truth.

By identifying my "false selves," naming them, befriending them, and eventually coming to terms with the wounds that created them, I hope to discover my authentic self. Ultimately I hope to accept that I don't need these "other selves" to protect me from pain. Without their interference, their pre-recorded messages, I can make mature, sound and relevant decisions based on the person I truly am, not who others want me to be. This is a way to nurture myself and cut the chains of slavery that bind me to others' ideas of who I should be.

I spend fruitful time reflecting on my false selves as I listen to the rain falling through the fir trees.

There is the Duchess, the belle of the ball who needs to be admired and loved by everyone, is above all the fray and will never show signs of hurt or anger. She sometimes finds it hard to accept that her once firm and youthful body is sagging, flabby, full of cellulite and wrinkles. She covers it up however she can.

There is St. Maureen of the Cloister: how virtuous and holy she is, not to mention wise and filled with grace. She obviously has a direct channel to God and is right there alongside Mother Teresa in her capacity for goodness.

Herculetta is a strong, capable, competent heroine, the best son my father ever had. There is little she cannot do successfully if she sets her mind and will to it.

Suzi Sunshine is my inner cheerleader; she keeps me trying when I'm ready to give in to fear and frustration. She means well but can be very irritating.

Cinderella is the frumpy, unloved, unappreciated girl with the heart of gold, mistreated by her sisters, unloved by her mother. She will do whatever anyone asks and can't say no. Some day a Prince Charming smart enough to see her true beauty will discover her, and then everyone will recognize her as the princess she is.

Finally, there is the Mother Who Lives Inside My Head. She is constantly judging me, telling me how inadequate I am on every score. Maybe the others are all trying to prove to her how wonderful we are.

An example of the confusion these selves bring is with money. The Duchess throws it about carelessly thinking she has an unending source. Cinderella has never had much, and she worries about spending money on anything she doesn't absolutely NEED. She wears stained clothing with holes or patches and hopes her wants and dreams will be fulfilled by someone else: a godmother or prince. And, of course, St. Maureen doesn't need money at all; she gives hers generously to others and good causes and feels holy as a result. The Mother points out how foolish everyone else is.

All these parts of me have a strong need to be loved, admired, and valued. I need to learn that what others think of me doesn't define me. Perhaps the only opinion about me that truly matters is my own. I know I am loved and lovable. I need to remember that, breathe it in, live from that reality. Ultimately, I am the one who must give myself the unconditional love and acceptance I crave. Connecting with the God Spirit within me, my own deepest longing, will assure me of my own intrinsic value and that of all creatures and creation.

While waiting for the Mo to have some regular service and repairs done, I hear about Care-a-Vanners, the Habitat for Humanity program developed for people with recreational vehicles who want to help build Habitat homes in different parts of the country. Care-a-Vanners has a Website listing builds available with places for RV volunteers to park free or very inexpensively. That piques my interest (or maybe it was St. Maureen who was intrigued): stay for a couple weeks with inexpensive rent, help construct a home for a needy family, learn a few skills, and investigate the area during my free time.

Aside from canoeing the Boundary Waters with Shirley, I have no definite plans. I recognize my discomfort with an open schedule and few specific destinations or dates. I need framework in my life. I want to see New England in the fall, so I start there and find a Habitat build in mid-September in Lewiston, Maine, that seems like a perfect choice.

I spend my last weekend in Portland attending my friend Julie's wedding and cantoring at Mass for the last time. Since the work on the Mo wasn't finished, I left it in the Eugene area and am staying at Troy's house where he gallantly gives me his bed and sleeps on an air mattress. He is my date for the wedding.

After picking up the Mo, it is time to say goodbye to my old life, to my city of Portland and venture out into the unknown. As I prepare to leave for at least two months with no sure knowledge of when I will be back, I feel anxious. I was in Europe for almost six weeks in 2005 but I didn't abandon my home and connections in Portland. This time, although I'm not going as far, I will leave no physical ties, only ties to my heart. I expect to return but am not certain if or when. I am leaving security and my known world behind, and stepping into the abyss. I feel as though I am venturing off on wild, storm-tossed waves that will bear me steadily away from the places and faces I love.

I have reservations to stay this first night in Eastern Washington, but beyond that, until I get to Minnesota some 2,000 miles away, I have no specific destinations. I push back the fear, resolving to deal with my insecurities and second-guessing one day at a time. I climb in the Mo, start the engine and begin my adventure as the miles roll away under my wheels.

‹※›

Chapter 6
Learning to Love Myself

We must be willing to get rid of the
life we've planned so as to have the
life that is waiting for us.
~ Joseph Campbell

I drive down the highway east into North Dakota singing along with Van Morrison, whose music I love. I have learned how to load my 10-CD player, which lasts a full day of driving. I particularly like this Morrison CD, *Avalon Sunset*. It is one John had bought; driving mostly empty freeways gives me the time to listen to the words of some of the songs. A number of them are very spiritual, one reason I'm so enamored of Morrison right now.

It is the third day since I left Portland following I-94 through Washington, Idaho and then Montana. I'm now in a state completely new to me, and I am impressed with how orderly it seems, at least viewed from the freeway.

The freeway is two perfectly parallel lines heading east-west. The distance between the two lines of pavement never seems to vary. The fields are huge but precise: an exact square of corn next to an exact square of wheat next to an exact square of alfalfa. Where the wheat has been harvested, the straw is cut in straight, neat rows waiting to be formed into huge round rolls. Even the hills are smoothed off, flat-topped or well rounded, unlike Montana's jagged peaks. Rows of trees planted between the fields hint of strong winds.

Fields of sunflowers look like tidy rows of grade school children sitting in a huge classroom, their bright faces all looking in the same direction (out the window at the sun, of course). Everything is green and lush, especially farther east where it's marshy.

Very few cars are on the freeway, maybe because they are all parked at one of the three rest stops waiting for the wind to stop blowing. It hasn't since I entered the state earlier today. Sunlight slips in and out of the clouds creating subtle changes in the color and texture of the landscape, and I run through rainstorms occasionally.

North Dakotans have a sense of humor, I think, driving past Salem Sue, the biggest Holstein in the world. She is a huge cow statue standing up on one of the hills. You can see her for miles from both east and west on the freeway. Funny thing is, though, I have not seen any Holsteins. The few cows I've seen have been Angus. North Dakota also proudly advertises the world's largest buffalo and the world's largest sandhill crane. I have yet to see live versions of those, either. I'm surprised they don't have the world's largest aardvark somewhere around here.

Another example of the North Dakota sense of humor: they close down one of the two freeway lanes for more than 20 miles for absolutely no reason. They're not doing any work. It's not torn up. Just close it down. What the heck! There's not that much traffic on a Monday (or probably any other day).

Marian's family came from the Dickinson area. Germans from Russia, the entire village moved from the Ukraine to North Dakota. That probably explains why everything is so meticulous here. If it were the Irish or Scots who settled here, things might have looked a bit different. Not necessarily better or worse, just different.

I'm following the route of the Lewis and Clark expedition. They wintered in 1804 in Mandan, just west of Bismarck, where Toussaint Pierre Charbonneau and his Shoshone wife Sacagawea joined them.

Morrison's "Have I Told You Lately" begins to play, bringing up competing memories. I suspect John bought this CD originally because of this song. He enjoyed browsing through used record stores and bringing home prizes; they often had love songs on them. I loved this song; John and I had often listened and danced to it. Now, when I don't skip it, I listen with tortured feelings. The other memories it stirs are nearly as painful as losing John, but in a different way, taking me back two years to when my heart was broken.

🛦🌟🛦

"Oh Charlie," I say as I rub his chin. When he sits next to me as I'm driving, he often rests his head on my leg and turns his face up to me. Golden retrievers have faces that convey a wide range of feelings. Right now Charlie is emitting "blissful" as he looks up at me with a little dog smile. He loves to be petted and especially appreciates it when I rub under his chin.

"Why didn't he love me?" I ask. As usual, Charlie is non-plussed. He doesn't get it either. Charlie thinks I am completely lovable, and the feeling is mutual. *Maybe you didn't give him enough bacon or dog treats*, Charlie's eyes seem to suggest.

Suddenly another voice chimes in.

"*It's been over two years. How long are you going to hold onto this pain, this betrayal?*" The Mother Who Lives inside My Head still hangs around to harass me from time to time, even though I have recognized her and tried to reconcile with her. Her comments sometimes hit the bulls-eye, a dart to my heart.

"Well, it hasn't been two years exactly."

"*Of course it has. It was two years ago that Lance chose someone else over you. How long are you going to insist on pining away for a man who obviously wasn't that interested in you? When will you accept that there is nothing for you there? He didn't want you.*"

"But it's only been a few months since we had that really great heart to heart talk," I remind her. It was a talk that had meant a lot to me in which he affirmed my value in his life and assured me that our relationship had been meaningful to him. "And it doesn't help that every time I see him he's friendly and flirty. And so darn cute."

"*Give me a break. He's friendly and flirty with most women.*"

I have to admit she's right.

"*Have you forgotten that he's married now?*"

"Of course not," I snap. "How can I forget something like that? That doesn't mean I can just forget him, just fall out of love with him." Bitch, I think to myself.

"*I am NOT a bitch,*" she says, reminding me she can read my mind. Of course she can; she IS my mind. "*I'm only trying to help you.*

"*I'm not sure what you ever saw in him in the first place,*" she continues to berate me. "*He never treated you right, took you for granted. You were just too damn nice to him and didn't stand up for yourself, didn't demand the respect you deserve.*"

"Yeah, I know. I was naïve," I admit. "But I was also in love with him. I have no idea why. All I know is that he is the one man I've met since John died for whom I would willingly give up my independence, my life even."

"*Such drama!*" she smirks. "*Know what I think? I think you like being the tragic heroine who falls in love with someone she can't have and pines her life away longing for him to come to his senses and return to her. I think you've read too many romance novels.*"

"Well, okay. Maybe that last part about giving my life WAS a little over the top. But you know I don't read romance novels," I say. "They're always so trite. Woman meets man, hates his guts, falls madly in love with him anyway and, after a contrived challenge or two, they live happily ever after. They have nothing in common with the lives of anyone I've ever known. Is there a happily ever after? I'd like to think so but it hasn't exactly been my experience."

"*Well, you really need to move on,*" she reminds me.

"I know, I know. Don't you think I know? Don't you think I've prayed about this? 'God, help me move past this man. Help me push these feelings away and never let them come to the surface again.' I almost get there and then something happens."

"Yeah, like you see him, or his car, or even a car that looks like his car, or you hear a song you listened to together, or remember something funny he said..."

"All right! I get it. You're right. You're always right. I'm trying, okay?" And I am. Part of the reason for this trip is to try to move beyond this pain. I really don't want to be a tragic heroine; I want to be a positive heroine: strong, wise, courageous and self-sufficient.

It's not like this is news to me, that I'm wasting my energy thinking about this love gone awry. This is typical of the conversations I have been having with myself for two years. The Mother always takes the logical, intelligent, strong road; I always fall into the ditches of self-pity along the sides of that road, getting slimy and dirty from wallowing and rolling in nostalgia and angst.

When I am driving, unless the traffic is intense, my mind has plenty of free time to wander down strange paths. I carry on long conversations with Charlie, with myself, with God. The Mother and I often rehash the same things over and over, with little progress toward resolution. The only thing we agree on is that I am hopeless. Neither of us wants to believe I am crazy; that would mean she is too, and she doesn't want to go there. We look for something else to argue about.

🌲🌵🌲

Often as my mind is wandering, I get little inspirations I try to remember later and write down. The Muse always comes to visit when I am in the middle of something and can't note her proffered inspirations. It would be fun to collect some of the very strange road names I've seen: Finnish School Road; Bear Butte Road; Old Swede Cannery Road (Sven and Ole beware). Funny little things that captivate my imagination and tickle my odd sense of humor. Perhaps I should have invested in a digital recorder when I got my Apple MacBook and my digital camera. But I have stretched my finances and technological abilities enough.

Sometimes I just watch the beautiful scenery roll by, or look at the small farmsteads and houses and wonder about the people who live there. I imagine what their lives are like and wonder what is important to them, what they believe in, whom they love; and that zaps me right back to Lance.

I met Lance several months after John's death when a mutual friend introduced us. Lance was the chief of staff for a state official in Salem, Oregon's capital, though he lived in Portland. Because of my work for the Senator, we traveled in the same professional circles and knew a number of people in common but had never met.

He had lost his wife and youngest son in a tragic accident. Both in our early 50s, we had unwillingly become members of a small, select group: people who have lost long-time spouses to traumatic sudden death. His loss was more recent than mine, and I hoped to support him through the painful minefield of grief.

"One of the difficult things for me about being single," I told him in one of our early conversations, "is not having someone to go do fun things with, like movies or dinner. If you ever want someone to just hang out with, go catch a movie or whatever, let me know."

All of my friends were married and had partners to do things with. Becoming single is a difficult transition. I no longer fit in; people seemed uncomfortable around me, like they weren't sure how to treat me, so I often felt overlooked or shut out. There seems to be a subtle exclusion of single women that many married women may not consciously realize.

Lance and I became friends and, in time, our shared pain and loneliness brought us much closer. As the weeks and months went by, I became convinced that God had brought us together so we could take care of each other. He made my grief easier to bear, and I believe I brought him a similar comfort.

He was just under 6′, lean but with well-defined muscles. He was attractive, with an endearing boyish charm that just missed being heartbreakingly handsome. He had a quiet confidence and a subtle sensuality. His coal hair with touches of gray, pale skin and deep blue eyes are what some describe as Black Irish. He was sweet and funny, supportive, gentle and unfailingly kind to me and everyone I ever saw him interact with.

Perhaps the best description of him is one he assigned to himself while telling me his favorite blend of Starbucks coffee:

"It's sweet but complex, kind of like me," he said.

"Well, you're definitely sweet," I said. "But you don't seem all that complex." I later discovered how accurate his self-assessment was. He was complex, non-committal and guarded, sometimes speaking in sound bites. From years of working in politics, he had learned to avoid directness and always weighed his words carefully. It was difficult to get a clear reading on his thoughts or to know him on a deep level.

He often teased me. One night, after he suggested for the fourth or fifth time "You should find a rich Republican," I told him with exasperation: "You know, I kinda like the guy I'm with right now!"

His comment stung. I wasn't sure if he was trying to be funny, was giving me a subtle warning that he didn't see a future with me because of my political affiliations, or if he truly thought I was so shallow I would be attracted to someone just because he had money.

While John and I had both been raised in conservative families, Lance came from a more liberal, activist background. He seemed mission-driven, trying to make a positive difference. His way of looking at the world helped me see through different filters and appreciate beauty in places I'd never thought to look before. Our conversations connected me with a more compassionate side of myself, one that was open and willing to look at all sides of an issue. His self-deprecating humor appealed to my silly, fun-loving side at a time when fun was hard to find. We enjoyed many of the same things and had similar beliefs and values. Being with him helped me grow and become a better person.

I treasured the limited time I was able to spend with him, and he seemed to enjoy being with me. He was affectionate and complimentary. He seemed to find me attractive and enjoy my company, and we shared amazing chemistry and passion.

He wasn't perfect, but I knew I was far from perfect myself. We were like two wounded birds, neither quite able to fly alone. But if we held each other tightly, leaned on each other, the two good wings between us allowed us to fly at least a little. Enough, I thought. He gave me hope and joy; and then he snatched it away, for reasons I have never really understood.

In retrospect, I realize my early marriage to John had given me little dating experience. There were plenty of hints and warning signs with Lance if I'd paid closer attention and been wiser. Maybe I just turned a blind eye to inconsistencies and doubts. Love will do that.

During the 15 months we were together, Lance avoided discussing his feelings about me, our relationship or anything that might even hint at a commitment or future. He declined to meet my children or friends and never introduced me to his family or friends. I suspect he told no one of our relationship or my role in his life. I didn't understand this secrecy; but respecting his need for discretion, I told very few of my friends about it. I loved him enough to give him the time and space he needed.

One evening Lance and I were sitting on my couch talking, and Morrison's *Avalon Sunset* was playing. When "Have I Told You Lately" came on, he asked me to change the music.

"That was our song," he explained with pain in his voice. "I'm still in love with her." I have never been able to listen to that song since without thinking of Lance and feeling first his pain, but later my own deep pain mixed with great tenderness and fondness.

Now as I drive east, another CD, *It's Time*, drops in and Michael Buble''s Sinatra-like voice is singing "Home," his hit song from a couple years earlier. It was popular when I was in Rome two summers ago. I listened to it while planning my trip to Europe, wishing Lance could go with me. I knew how much I was going to miss him; I had fallen in love with him.

⁂

Before John's accident, Kristin had been planning her wedding for the following summer. A few weeks after saying our goodbyes to John, we were talking about the wedding.

"This is so hard, mom," she said. "There is so much to do, and I can't decide where to hold the wedding, and there are so many things that need to be planned. And now I don't have my dad to walk me down the aisle. This is just too stressful." She began sobbing.

"Oh, I know, honey, and I'm so sorry. What about finding a place you and Ryan want to go to, and just having a small family wedding?" I suggested. "Then we can have a reception for friends and family after we get back."

I was thinking about Hawaii which Kristin had long held a desire to visit. She was the most traveled in our family, having visited Germany and Australia. I had gotten my first passport only a year earlier.

"I'll see what Ryan thinks," she said, brightening.

Ryan thought we should go to Italy, specifically Tuscany. Ryan had studied in Siena during college. He wanted Kristin to see it. I was delighted Italy would be the wedding destination; I had always yearned to travel there.

Kristin and Ryan found a villa outside of Siena and scheduled their wedding for early June of 2005. Though I tried to talk Lance into coming for at least part of the trip, he declined.

Visiting Italy and then Switzerland, France and Ireland was a dream come true for me. My sisters joined me separately, each for about three weeks so I had company on my travels. Being away from loved ones for six weeks was difficult. I knew Charlie was in good hands with my brother Tom and that he had Nick for company, but I missed him and knew he would be missing me.

Most of all, though, I missed Lance. I emailed him several times and called him from Switzerland. I came home bearing gifts for him. I didn't know that while I was exploring Europe, he was exploring another relationship. I had no clue what was awaiting me when I flew back into Portland. I was anxious to see Lance and disappointed when he wasn't at the airport and didn't answer my calls.

Lance returned my call the following day and arranged to see me that night. I greeted him warmly—it felt so good to see him again, to hold him. After briefly telling him about my trip, I leaned back against him and started to tell him how much I had missed him and how very happy I was to be with him again. He stiffened, nudged me away and said he needed to tell me something.

"I've met someone. It's not fair to her or to you for me to continue to see both of you."

I was stunned. All I could do was pat him on the leg and say, "It's okay, it's okay." St. Maureen was trying to console him and, at the same time, trying to convince me that it actually was going to be okay. The Mother wanted to slap him and yell: *"You stupid idiot! You fool! What is wrong with you? I love you. Don't you get that?"* But St. Maureen remained in control: kind, calm and self-sacrificing.

As he walked out my door, I gave him one last hug. "I wish this weren't happening. I like you so very much," I said. He choked back a sob as he said goodbye.

I spent that night unable to sleep, feeling as though someone had stabbed me in the heart with an icy dagger, letting all my hope and joy and spirit leak out. It was another loss to mourn, but this time so few people knew of our relationship there was no outpouring of love and sympathy, help and support.

The few friends who knew about us assured me I was better off, saying things like: "He never appreciated how lucky he was to have you," and "Always remember, it's his loss." I wanted to hate him, and sometimes I did briefly, but I couldn't see the scoundrel they saw. I saw a confused man whose own shattered heart hadn't yet healed. My hopes of helping him heal were replaced by the pain of knowing he'd chosen someone else. I saw a man I loved deeply and knew this loss would be harder for me in some ways. John would never have left me intentionally; Lance had.

We had agreed to remain friends, and we both tried to make that happen. We were cordial and kind to each other. It was inevitable that I would see him occasionally; when I did it was exquisite torture, joy mingled with pain. The first time I saw them together, holding hands, it felt like a violent kick in the stomach. I tried to let him go emotionally while still being friends, a difficult challenge I barely had the strength for.

Despite the sadness I felt when I heard of their marriage several months ago, I told myself at least I could move on. It was clear he would never be in my life again as he had once been. I knew it was the end of the first chapter of my new book of life.

"Apparently you're having some problems turning the page," the Mother points out. *"You do realize you can't put your happiness in*

*anyone else's hands, don't you? You're the only one who can control
your life, your joy, and your fulfillment."*

"You're right! I just have to strengthen my wings so I can fly
alone."

🝔🝔🝔

"There were good things, though," I muse over a glass of wine
after Charlie and I are settled for the night somewhere in North
Dakota. "He taught me so much and opened my eyes and heart in
many ways.

"And at least I know I can fall in love, even if Lance wasn't the
right one. Maybe there will be another man some day; maybe I can fall
in love again." Assuming I can fall out of love with this guy, I think.

Throughout my life I had worried there was something lacking in
my emotional makeup that prevented me from experiencing the
intense passion that I understood as falling in love. This subject had
been of great interest and concern to me, and I often questioned friends
who talked about being in love. How do you know, what does it feel
like? I had loved John deeply, and his absence in my life continues to
be painful. Maybe the kind of love I had for John—warm glowing
embers rather than roaring flames—was more practical, more realistic,
and possibly a more solid foundation to build a life on.

My deep love for Lance gave me the strength to wish him
happiness, despite my own loneliness and the pain I felt in losing him.
It allowed me to forgive the hurt and continue to love him in spite of
what felt like betrayal.

In acknowledging the depth of the feelings I had for Lance—still
have—I realize I do not feel that way about Troy, not even remotely.
Having now experienced those feelings, I want to hold out for them
and not settle for less. I deserve to fall in love again, with someone
who loves me back.

One of my spiritual directors had talked about falling in love with
God. Maybe my new understanding of love can lead me to fall in love
with my Creator, who loves me far more deeply and passionately than
any other being. It is time to focus on the most important relationships
in my life: with myself and with my God.

꙼꙼꙼

Chapter 7
Taking Shortcuts

If all difficulties were known at
the outset of a long journey, most
of us would never start out at all.
~ Dan Rather

Minnesota is my first major destination on the cross-country trip. I arrive in Prior Lake at my sister's home on the afternoon of August 7, four days after leaving Portland. I had visited Shirley here for several days the Christmas following John's death. Walking across a frozen lake to visit a fishing shack and seeing cars and trucks parked on the ice was a disconcerting first for me. My hair freezing as we sat in a hot-tub led us to visit Cabo San Lucas the following Christmas.

Shirley is nearly 16 years younger than me, but we have been close for many years. Her landlord, Tim, provided me with a place to park the Mo next to the house.

Tim is a welder and has a full shop. I tell him I need 50-amp service, and he is happy to oblige. However, when I try to hook up the electricity, the plugs don't match.

"Hey, we can fix this," Tim says, full of confidence. "I'll just go see my friend over at the hardware store. He'll have the parts we need."

"Tim likes to hang out at the hardware store," Shirley explains after he leaves. "I'm sure he's glad to have an excuse to go over there and shoot the breeze."

True to his word, Tim returns with all the parts and refits his electrical plug. I am so caught up envying and admiring his ability to rewire the plug, it doesn't occur to me there might be a good reason the plugs don't match.

It has been unusually dry in Minnesota this summer. When I arrive most of the ponds are patches of mud, the lakes are low and full of algae. Even with a drought, Minnesota is beautifully green but unmercifully humid. However, in honor of my presence, the weather gods decide to send the long-awaited rains and, one night, the most traumatic thunderstorm I've ever experienced.

It begins between 2 and 3 a.m. with a bright flashing sky, rumbling, booming and crashing. The wind is wild and the rain pours. Often the lighting flashes are constant—no seconds of darkness for comfort between them. The Mo shakes with the winds, and I quake with fear that the big cottonwood tree I am parked under will come crashing down. I finally crawl into the bathroom, shut the doors and cower on the floor, holding Charlie. Fortunately, he remains calm and sane, a solid force to comfort me. I huddle there for what seems like hours, hiding behind my pillows, with wild violence roaring outside my little womb that feels neither safe nor strong. I beg God to keep me safe and send the storm on its way.

Finally around 5 the thunder and lightning diminish, and I slink back into bed. I wake late the next morning, to cooler, cleaner air and ponds beginning to look like ponds instead of mud wallows. I am exhausted from lack of sleep and drained by fear and apprehension. Surviving that storm reminds me how much I value my life; I need to move forward with that in mind. When I get lazy or complacent or nervous about the next step, I can relive the experience of the thunderstorm and remember my strong will to continue on with my life, my journey.

Between storms, Shirley and I spend time visiting, riding bikes, taking a couple of boat tours of Prior Lake, attending the St. Paul Irish festival, hiking and getting ready for our trip to the Boundary Waters. We take Charlie out in a rental canoe to see how he rides, unsure whether to take him along to the Boundary Waters. Once we manage to get him into the canoe, he moves from side to side trying to drink the water. I finally get him to lie down in the bottom of the canoe a couple times, and once he even stays for almost five minutes. But I realize we will have enough stress going out into the wilderness in canoes without having a dog tipping the boat.

We meet Shirley's friend Jan, who has invited us to join her family in this canoe adventure, and discuss things we need to bring. Jan and Jim have canoed the Boundary Waters numerous times before.

We prepare and freeze the food for the meal we are contributing. We borrow a canoe from Tim's brother. I buy a sleeping bag and a few other supplies I will need. We will use Shirley's tent and air mattress. All our clothing and personal articles have to fit into a very small day-pack, and the daypacks, sleeping bags, tent, food and boxes of wine all have to fit into the Duluth bag, which is supposedly waterproof.

Monday, after a stormy weekend, we drive north to Grand Rapids, Minn., to meet Jan, Jim and their sons. Sam, the oldest and a Marine, has been recently commissioned as an officer after serving in Afghanistan. Matt and John are both college students, and Matt's girlfriend Samantha is joining us. We spend the night at a cabin Jim and Jan own on the shores of a small lake.

Tuesday morning we drive to Ely, the main jumping-off point for entering the Boundary Waters Canoe Area Wilderness, a million acres of interlocking lakes and streams, with 1,500 miles of mapped canoe routes but no roads or modern conveniences. It is the largest wilderness preserve in the eastern U.S. and attracts canoers, kayakers and wilderness enthusiasts from all over North America. The area stretches along the border between northeastern Minnesota and Ontario, Canada, hence the name "Boundary Waters."

After getting the necessary permits, we drive several miles to the offloading site for Lakes 1, 2, 3 and 4. By this time, the gas gauge on Shirley's car shows a nearly empty fuel tank. We park, unload the canoes and carry them 50 yards down to the water. Then we carry the Duluth bags, each weighing about 80 pounds, down and stow them into the canoes. We settle into our canoes and head off into our wilderness adventure. Shirley and I are the only all-woman canoe, and I am the only inexperienced paddler.

We follow a beautiful stream filled with blooming water lilies before hitting open water. We portage across a fairly narrow spit of land between two of the lakes. I'm not happy we have to portage, which requires a couple of trips carrying the canoe—a two-person job unless you are a strong Marine; carrying the paddles and life preservers and other smaller pieces of equipment; strapping the huge Duluth bag on your back and crawling camel-like across the trail. So many people are traversing the well-worn, level trail it feels downright crowded for a remote area.

Resuming paddling, we travel through the first two lakes and into the third. We decide to try a vacant campsite that looks like it will accommodate four tents on an island in Lake 3. If we don't like it, we can find a different site tomorrow.

The site has a large log near the fire pit that serves as a counter for preparing food and doing dishes. It has plenty of room for all our tents, hammocks and tarps in case it rains, and we have the island to ourselves. Except for another camp across the lake and occasional paddlers passing by in the middle of the lake, we are a solitary tribe of eight people.

These are the roughest living conditions I've experienced since I was a Camp Fire Girl and we had to dig our own latrine. Fortunately, we are spared that indignity here; the comfort station is a toilet seat perched over a pit, the only privacy provided by thick brush and a few hundred yards distance from the campsite.

We have no electricity. We haul water up from the middle of the lake adding Kool-Aid to disguise the taste. Kool-Aid doesn't do much to eliminate germs, and I worry about giardia, but Jan and Jim and their family have done this for years and they are still alive so I try not to stress about it. Everything we need, except firewood and water, we carried in.

The next two days we relax. In between cooking and cleaning up, we paddle out to explore the lake and fish or, in my case, try to capture the perfect photo. To the disappointment of those fishing, no fish are killed or injured; though Shirley catches one fish, she feels merciful and returns it to the lake.

We have time to read, visit, sit on the bank and gaze out at the water and the distant shorelines, watch the sunset, admire the beauty, and sit around the campfire at night laughing with friends and watching the awesome stars and meteor showers. With no light pollution, we see stars and galaxies that are invisible from less remote sites. Surrounded by water, trees, wide blue skies, and a deep quiet, we feel an unearthly peacefulness. The grandeur of this natural beauty, day and night, far exceeds anything humans could conceive and build.

These days have been a lesson in living in the present. There is little that needs to be done, no television, no computer, no phones, no cars; we can't go anywhere except paddling, and there is no place we need to be. It is a wonderful gift to just be, just enjoy the moment, without guilt. It is a reminder that, in reality, all we have is now, this moment. I know that better than most people; tomorrow, if it comes, is likely to be very different than I imagine or dream.

During our stay we also consume some 23 liters of wine—for medicinal purposes, of course. The men are very quiet until they've imbibed a little. On the last night we need to finish off the wine so we won't have to haul any back. Of course, it would be sacrilegious for good Catholics to throw wine out, and it could hurt the fish. As we sit around the campfire, relaxed and cozy, Sam begins to read Viking poetry from a book of Icelandic tales. It is a perfect, if rather strange and unexpected, ending to this surreal time. As I make my way to the tent for my last night of roughing it, I reflect on this family—complete strangers to me a few days ago—and know I will never forget them or this experience they allowed me to share.

🌲🌿🌲

"The winds are really rough today and crossing over that open water with the wind against us would be a lot of work. I've been studying the map and this looks like a route we could take that would be a shortcut and eliminate some of the open water." Jim points to the map.

He, Sam, Matt and John are discussing the pros and cons of striking out on an alternate course as we prepare to leave our island home of the last three days and return to civilization. We all look at the map and agree it appears to be a reasonable route that doesn't require portaging. It also should cut off several miles of paddling across wide lakes. We are tired and anxious to get back to modern conveniences, bathe in hot water, do laundry and use flush toilets.

I'm always in favor of an easier way, but I am also old and wise enough to know that shortcuts aren't always shorter or easier. Besides, the maps don't always show which routes are actually passable by canoe, and the navigable areas change depending on rain and water levels. It is mid-August of a dry summer. There might be a reason this shortcut is not marked as a canoe trail.

We dismantle our tents, roll our sleeping bags and stuff everything into the Duluth bags. Loading up our canoes, we set off across water reflecting a deep blue sky, placing our trust in the hands of these new friends.

After crossing the lake we enter a lovely river. We soon discover, however, that because of the drought, the river is full of rapids and many boulders hide just below the surface of the water. Shirley and I have the heaviest canoe with the deepest draft and the only canoe without a strong, strapping man with Boundary Waters experience, though we do have Herculetta and her sister, Shirwecan.

As we maneuver through the rocks, our canoe runs aground. We push against the rocks with our paddles, using all our strength and undoubtedly uttering a few swear words—at least I am—and finally push the canoe free. Minutes later we are caught on another rock. As we push with all our might, one of the paddles cracks and half of it goes floating down the river.

In spite of our efforts, we are making no headway, so out of sheer frustration Herculetta climbs out and tries to push the canoe off the rock. I am wearing my life jacket and don't consider the possibility of stepping into a deep hole or slipping on slick rocks. Eventually it is free, and I climb back into the canoe without tipping it. We borrow a spare paddle from one of the other canoes and continue on.

This scenario plays out several more times as we make our way slowly through rapids filled with treacherous rocks, though we avoid breaking more paddles. I am soaked from my chest down but fortunately our canoe remains upright and our things—as well as Shirley—are still relatively dry.

Sam and John have been leading us and are scouting out the stream ahead. They gather us together to warn that a series of rapids just ahead looks too difficult for even the most experienced, strongest paddlers. We need to portage. Or turn back and go the way we came. This is unwelcome news, and given the struggles we've already overcome, and the fact that we would have to retrace our steps and be paddling against the current, we agree to portage. Sometimes it's less daunting to continue forward in life than go backwards.

We paddle to shore and unload everything from the canoes while the men explore a route. They return with the news that there is a faint though steep path. They offer to carry the canoes; the women will bring everything else. Normally one strong person can put a canoe on his or her shoulders and carry it alone. This portage is so rough it requires two people on a canoe so it takes two trips to get all four of the canoes through the portage.

As the men set off with the first two canoes, I hoist our Duluth bag onto my shoulders, staggering with the weight. I use two paddles as walking sticks to help balance the load. The path is very rough, sometimes hard to follow or even discern, and is questionable at best for portaging. I struggle but am making it, until I come to a tree that has fallen across the path at waist height. I can't fit under it with the huge pack on my back and I can't climb over. I take the pack off, balancing it on the log as I scramble over, then put it back on and continue along the tortuous route. I have no idea how others are faring.

Nearing the site where we will reload the canoes, I step onto the base of an old stump and suddenly my leg plunges into a hole, bruising and scraping my knee badly. With help from Shirley I escape the clutches of the forest and finish the portage. It ends with a steep climb up over rocks and then a drop down to the bank that is so sheer we tie ropes onto the Duluth bags and lower them down rather than trying to carry them. Personally I'd be happy to pitch them down.

The men have reentered the water a little upstream and have a final set of rapids to negotiate before bringing the canoes to our landing site. When we have everything portaged and ready to load, we find vantage points and watch Sam and John maneuver the last canoe through the rapids. Even empty and with skilled paddlers, we hold our breath and pray the canoe doesn't tip.

Everyone cheers as the last canoe is brought to the bank, and we begin to stow our gear, ready to make the last leg. We are relieved that we have avoided any major accidents, tipping canoes, loss of equipment or serious injury and pray there are no more portages. Shirley gets into the canoe as I steady it for her, then I prepare to climb board. I lift my leg over the side while Shirley counterbalances. Suddenly, the canoe shifts and flips. Instantly I am in the water, my uninjured knee striking a rock as I go down. Shirley and our gear all land in the water.

We grab the canoe, right it and rescue the paddles before the current takes them out of reach.

"Oh my God, I'm so sorry," I sputter as together we drag our Duluth bag out of the river and roll it back into the canoe. "I have no idea how that happened. I'm sorry."

Truthfully it's probably just a great stroke of luck or a major miracle that it hasn't happened sooner.

Once the dripping equipment is settled back into the canoe, Shirley and I, soaked, frustrated and on the verge of exhaustion, climb back aboard and set off.

We make it through The Shortcut, which probably took two hours longer than if we'd returned the way we came. But the guys have had a good adventure and challenge. We paddle back across Lake 1 struggling against the wind. When we finally arrive at the landing spot where we'd left the cars, I want to fall down on my knees and kiss the ground—except that both my knees are bruised and bleeding.

In spite of the challenges of the last few hours, I am glad I made this trip. I feel the deep satisfaction that comes from meeting adversity and overcoming it, realizing that I have gumption. I can be strong—and stubborn—enough to handle life if I take it one moment, one crisis, at a time, as long as I don't allow my negative thoughts and fear to keep me from trying.

That prehistoric part of my brain, the fear center known as the amygdala, often sends out false alarms, and when I listen to those, I am reacting to an out-of-order alarm system. It's always on Red Alert. Martha Beck calls this the "lizard brain." Mine is named Hazel, after my maternal grandmother who, though a sweet and wonderful lady, was a bit of a hypochondriac who lived her life fearing she had heart problems. She outlived all three of her children, dying in her mid-90s.

In addition to realizing my own ability to persevere, I have been amazed and impressed with the strength of character, as well as the physical strength, of everyone else on the trip. After we land the canoe, I am struggling to put the Duluth bag on my shoulders to carry it to the car. Sam comes by already carrying a Duluth bag.

"Need some help?" he offers.

"Can you just help me get it lifted up onto my shoulders?" I say thankfully. With one hand, he picks the bag up and carries it up the hill, depositing it by our car as easily as if it weighs only eight pounds. Darn show-off!

After hugs and thanks all around, Shirley and I set off in search of a gas station. We are soaked and cold, but dig through our packs and find some mostly dry clothes for the trip home.

We had considered driving home through Duluth to visit Shirley's friends who are camping on Lake Superior. Because of our damp clothes and damper spirits, we head back to Prior Lake. I miss the chance to put my toe in Lake Superior, but accept that cheerfully, realizing I've had enough of lakes to last me for at least a few days.

I am anxious to get back to see how Charlie fared with Tim.

Chapter 8
Restoring Power

There is only one journey.
Going inside yourself.
~ Rainer Maria Rilke

My blog for August 19 contains photos of the Boundary Waters with an accompanying comment that they "are nicer than pictures of me crying."

I haven't actually been crying—that in itself is pretty amazing given the news that greets me back in Prior Lake. I haven't been screaming, either; just swearing very quietly. The good news is Charlie is fine and happy to see me. The bad news is a disaster.

"I dunno what's goin' on with your motor home," Tim starts to explain. "There's somethin' wrong with the electricity. It's been so hot here. So couple days ago me and Tom were sittin' in there with the air conditioner running, havin' a couple beers, when everything just stopped. I checked the plugs and everything's still hooked up.

"I got a friend who sells motor homes," he continues, "so I talked to her and her husband. They think maybe we got it hooked up to the wrong voltage."

Aha! Maybe that's why the plugs didn't fit together and had to be converted, I realize, too late. I can't really blame Tim for hooking me up to 220 volts instead of the 110 my motor home requires. I wouldn't know the difference, since electrical circuitry is not one of my hobbies. In fact, it's another of those deep, dark mysteries of life, right up there with how diesel engines work or how a man thinks.

The bottom line is, something happened and I have no electricity in the Mo. Finding fault or casting blame won't change that. Figuring out how to fix it will take all the energy I have left.

Taking advantage of the two-hour time difference between Minnesota and Oregon, I call the service department where I've had work done before. It's Friday night and I don't expect much so am ecstatic when a technician answers. I explain the problem.

"There's several possibilities," he begins. "Sounds like you could have blown out the inverter." I have never quite figured out exactly what this little machine does, but I think it converts the DC current to AC for most efficient use by the motor home.

"It's possible it might also have blown the microwave, and maybe the television, or the air conditioner. Or you might have to replace all the appliances," he says.

I groan and utter a few choice words, mostly under my breath. But there's more: "The inverter alone will probably cost about $2,500 to replace, but sometimes you can get your insurance to pay part of that."

Lord, thank you for this tiny little silver lining for a black cloud.

I call the Monaco Service number to see if they can recommend a service department in the Twin Cities. I get no answer and will probably have to wait until Monday to talk with them. The prospect of no electricity disturbs me, despite having just survived three days and nights in the wilderness with no modern conveniences whatever.

I take a long, hot shower in Shirley's bathroom, borrow a battery-powered lantern and head to bed in the dark. At least I'm sleeping on a bed again instead of an air mattress, and Charlie is by my side.

Before ending my day I call Troy to let him know I returned from the wilderness. It is supposed to be up to me to make contact, though he hasn't lived up to our agreement and has called me several times for long conversations since I left Portland, running up my cell phone bill.

"Hey, we had a great trip to the Boundary Waters," I tell him, and recount our adventures. His young adult daughter was canoeing with friends the week before, coming out the day we went in.

"But there seems to be something wrong with the electricity on the motor home," I mention. I do not ask for his help or advice, I am only sharing my frustrations with him regarding yet another hurdle I've encountered. I explain what I think is going on with the Mo.

"Do you have Triple A?" he asks, immediately jumping into rescue mode. "They can probably come help you. I have a friend in the Minneapolis area. I'll call him. Maybe he can help."

"I don't have Triple A; I don't really think they could help in this situation. I've made some calls and have it pretty well under control. I just have to wait until the service places open Monday. I really don't need you to make any calls for me, but thanks for offering."

Saturday I try Monaco Service again and am able to talk with a technician. He suggests I try starting the generator. I go out to the front of the Mo, prime the engine and push the start button. Nothing.

"Ooooh, boy! That doesn't sound good," he says. "I think you might have some serious problems." No kidding, I think to myself.

He gives me the names and phone numbers of several certified repair places in the Minneapolis area. I call them all but none are open. Tim and I spend much of the rest of the day trying to figure out the problem. Something in me won't let me just sit around and wait for help to arrive. In a traffic jam I'd rather get off the freeway and find a way through surface streets; even if it takes longer I feel I'm making progress instead of sitting and waiting helplessly. I'd better never get lost in the woods.

Troy calls and tells me he's spoken with Triple A about getting some help for me. He's also talked with a friend who is a mechanical engineer to get his suggestions. His apparent assumption that I'm incapable of solving my own problems irritates me, though I don't call him on his interference.

"It's okay," St. Maureen whispers to me. *"He's only trying to help. Don't get angry. You're probably completely misreading it anyway."*

"No," I argue back, "he's treating me like a helpless female who needs rescuing, and that's insulting. He has no idea how to fix a motor home or even the source of my problems. He's never owned or driven a motor home. I doubt Triple A, even if I had coverage, would be able to help me in this situation."

"Well, okay," she says, *"but don't get angry. Take a breath and just let it go. He doesn't mean anything by it other than that he cares about you and wants to help."*

"Whatever," I say, dismissing her but taking a deep breath.

"Thanks," I say to Troy, "I appreciate your trying to help, but like I said, I have some calls in, and I have a pretty good idea how to get this fixed. I'll keep you posted." St. Maureen wins this round. But I'm inclined to avoid talking to him again until I have it resolved.

What is it about men that they think they have all the answers, even when they're more than a thousand miles away? Knights are great to have around if you are trying to vanquish infidels or battle a serious dragon problem, but sometimes people need to stretch enough to take care of their own problems and not be rescued. It's how we grow and develop more confidence. Is this something he doesn't understand, or does he not want me to grow and become more confident? Yes, he's nice but nice truly isn't the be all and end all of a relationship partner. He seems to lack trust and confidence in me.

Again I get the sense that Troy is patting me on the head like I'm a helpless, silly little child who needs an adult male to protect her. He has indicated subtly he doesn't agree with my need to take this journey, but being magnanimous, he is going along with it. Now he seems to suggest that I am not competent or capable enough to complete what I set out to do. That pretty much tells me everything I need to know about a future with Troy, though I postpone making any final decisions and ending the relationship. I have enough on my plate right now without thinking about relationships.

I often wonder if these challenges I encounter are temptations to make me abandon this pilgrimage. That convinces me it is even more important to continue and ignore thoughts of quitting. In my heart I know I am not a quitter, and pushing me only makes my Irish take over and hardens my resolve.

I have discovered a steel core inside myself that keeps me standing straight in adversity. I can be flexible when necessary, but giving up or falling apart or despairing don't work. I might allow myself to wallow in self-pity for a little while, but am likely to grit my teeth and come up swinging when I've regained my strength.

When dangerous waves come your way in a canoe or kayak, you are supposed to meet them head on—actually face into them—to avoid getting capsized. This seems like a good metaphor for many of life's unexpected challenges: keep your eyes open, face your fears and move into them with courage and strength.

This is another challenge to face in my voyage of self-discovery. In the past I have chosen the easier path, avoiding challenge. Take the downhill trail, I told myself. Uphill is too hard, and you really didn't want to see the view anyway. If the struggle was too great, I assumed it wasn't the right path for me. But it is time for me to face life's challenges head-on.

🌲🦋🌲

Monday morning I phone one of the repair places Monaco has referred me to and arrange to take the Mo to Lakeland Coach in nearby Burnsville. After checking out the systems, they tell me too much voltage has fried the inverter, and it needs to be replaced. They order a replacement inverter. They can make the repairs as soon as it arrives. We won't know how the appliances fared until the inverter is installed and working.

Waiting for the inverter to arrive gives me a few extra days with Shirley and keeps me in Minnesota for my birthday. It is a rare treat to spend my birthday with her. If not for the repairs, I would have been alone on my birthday, undoubtedly feeling lonely and sorry for myself.

Shirley and I talk about my travels and my ongoing challenges to keep moving forward.

"You are so fortunate to be able to do this, Maureen," she admonishes me. "Don't give it up. See this through."

"Why don't you come with me, at least for a while?" I suggest. "It would really be fun. We could explore some old Civil War battlefields, and you could probably get continuing education credit." She'd been laid off from her job teaching history and social studies in the spring and hadn't yet found another position. She hesitates to leave without having a job to return to. I understand that. She has to rely on herself. She probably also recognizes the importance of this time of solitude for me. Even though she is much younger than I, she is very wise.

We also talk about relationships, and I share my doubts about the future of my relationship with Troy.

Again she counsels: "If you don't see this going anywhere, you need to tell him. It's not fair to keep him on a string, keep him thinking there's something there when there isn't. And the sooner you do that, the better. Then you can both move on. Don't treat him like Lance treated you when you have no interest in a long-term relationship." Zing! She knows how to get to my underbelly.

"Well, I'm not positive," I say, hedging. "There are some really good things about him. But this whole issue of him jumping in and trying to rescue me really ticks me off. He needs to back way off. And he needs to quit calling me and give me this time alone."

"Then you need to tell him that," she says.

She's right, and I will. Soon. Really!

✿

Chapter 9
Heading Farther East

Accomplish the journey beyond
yourself and reach God.
~ Rumi

O n August 23, the second day of my 58th year, and 16 days, two badly scarred knees and $1,200 after arriving in Minnesota, my journey continues. None of the appliances in the Mo were affected and the inverter was rebuilt, saving about half the estimated cost. This mistake could have been much costlier. I will talk with my insurance company about getting some of it reimbursed.

Saying goodbye to Shirley and Tim, I drive east into Wisconsin. It's been more than two weeks since I've driven the Mo, and I always feel nervous starting out again, but it all comes back quickly. I feel rested, tested and ready to face the challenges of being a single woman exploring this beautiful country.

My next destination is Green Bay and Door County, a picturesque peninsula that juts out into Lake Michigan. Seven hours after leaving Burnsville, I reach Sturgeon Bay, home for the next few nights.

While here I will visit a friend who now lives in Green Bay. I met Tony when I worked for a small weekly tabloid in Portland 20 years earlier. Through his guidance and support, what started as a part-time clerical job became a fulfilling career. Working with Tony on the newspaper helped me recognize my talent and love for writing. In my mid-30s, working 30 hours a week and with two young children, I returned to college and completed my degree in communications.

Tony later became the editor of the diocesan newspaper in Green Bay, and we kept in touch. He always sends outrageously funny Christmas letters about life in Green Bay. I half expect to see the remains of last winter's snow under the shade trees or a snow blower parked on their roof when I visit him, his wife Jackie and their dog, Jasmine, who often stars in those Christmas letters. I will join them

Saturday evening for dinner at their home. In the meantime, I explore the miles of coastline and little harbor towns.

Large barns and silos dominate the Wisconsin skyline, but there are plenty of trees and even hills in this part of the state. Cornfields are scattered among the green pastures and dairies.

Just as North Dakota is surprisingly adept at humor, Wisconsin does cute quite well.

Charlie and I wander through the charming towns of Egg Harbor, Fish Creek, Sister Bay and Bailey's Harbor. Door County is known as the Cape Cod of the Midwest; it's nautical and touristy with a variety of shops in large old buildings or tiny cottages. I have Charlie along so I don't do any shopping, undoubtedly saving money. I have not forgotten the lesson learned from selling (or giving away) so many of my things in May.

Sailboats and powerboats are tied to the docks and anchored in the bays. People with time, money and a love of boating could have a grand summer harbor hopping on Lake Michigan and Green Bay.

We wade in both the Green Bay and Lake Michigan sides of the peninsula. The water is very clear—I expected it to be less clean—and surprisingly warm. Charlie is his usual charming self and several small children pet him.

This part of Wisconsin is about 100 miles from Waukesha, the town where John spent a year of college attending a Catholic seminary before we met. This is not the first time thoughts of John have accompanied me on this trip we dreamed about doing together.

Just up the road from the RV park is a farm stand. I buy fresh corn, peaches, tomatoes and a small bottle of maple syrup. This area is known for its cherries, but we are well past cherry season. I look forward to a summer meal of fresh corn on the cob and sliced tomatoes with peaches and cream for dessert. I don't have the luxury of having a garden so farm stands will have to do.

When we return to the RV park, the couple "next door" is sitting under their awning.

"What a beautiful dog!" says the woman. I'm always happy to share Charlie so I walk him over to say hello.

"This is Charlie," I say. "I'm Maureen."

"We used to have goldens, years ago," she says, introducing herself as Colette. "We miss them—they're such wonderful dogs! But when our last one died we decided not to get another dog. We've been full-timers for about four years now, and having a large dog in a motor home is challenging."

"Seems once people have had a golden retriever, they can't pass by one without stopping to talk to both the dog and his person," I play with Charlie's soft ear as he leans against me. "And he does take a lot of room and time, but I'd be lost without Charlie for company. We're traveling across the country together. I'm trying to figure out what to do with my life now that I'm a widow."

"Is it safe?" Colette worries. "Do you ever feel afraid?"

"Well, that's one of the benefits of having a big dog. Even if he would probably never hurt a soul, he has a loud, deep bark that sounds threatening. I haven't felt uncomfortable or in danger yet. And really, if push comes to shove, I think he would protect me and his home." Unless, I think to myself, the threatening person has doggie treats.

Colette tells me she and her husband Wayne are from Colorado, although they are "registered" in Texas. They will eventually winter in South Carolina.

"I'm planning to be in Maine by mid-September. There's a Habitat for Humanity build I've signed up to help with," I say. "But then I may spend the winter in Florida. I want to visit a good friend just outside of Jacksonville."

"Why don't you think about traveling with us?" Colette suggests when she realizes we have similar itineraries. "We'll be going through New York and New England, then Pennsylvania before we get to the Carolinas. I'm worried about you traveling alone."

"Wow, that is really nice of you and pretty tempting," I say. "Thank you for offering to let me tag along. It would be great to have the company, at least for part of the time. The loneliness—doing everything alone—is my biggest challenge."

We compare notes about our plans, but they will be arriving in Maine about the time I need to be back in Oregon for John's memorial scholarship fundraiser. Their RV memberships don't mesh with mine so staying in the places they stay would cost me more.

"Dang, I just don't see how this will work, but it would have been really nice."

Colette hands me their family business card. "When you get to South Carolina, give us a call and come visit. We'll probably be there by early November."

🌲🌼🌲

Saturday night Charlie stays in the Mo while I drive into Green Bay for dinner with Tony and Jackie.

"Where you heading next?" Tony asks as he offers me more pasta.

"North. I'll drive around Lake Michigan up to St. Ignace, maybe visit Mackinac Island. So weird that little area is part of Michigan, which it doesn't look like it's even connected to, instead of Wisconsin.

That would make more sense." I decline the pasta but help myself to salad.

"Just so you don't sound like a tourist, it's pronounced 'mackinaw.' And there's an interesting story about how Michigan became the proud owner of that not-so-coveted piece of lakefront property.

"When state lines were laid out in the 1830s, both Ohio and Michigan wanted what was known as the Toledo strip, the area on Lake Erie south of Detroit. This led to the Toledo War, which was finally settled when Michigan agreed to accept the Upper Peninsula instead.

"This turned out to be wise, since the Upper Peninsula's mines produced nearly all of America's copper in the second half of the 19th century and became the largest supplier of iron ore. A lot of wealth came out of an area that, at one point, no one seemed to want."

Tony is a font of obscure and quirky information like that.

I mention that every little town I've seen in Wisconsin seems to have a Catholic church.

"Because of the harsh winters, the diocese built churches about every seven miles. Now there are too many churches and not enough priests, or Catholics to fill them, so they're combining parishes."

After my visit with Tony, I study atlases preparing to leave for Michigan tomorrow. It's late August, and I haven't made reservations for Labor Day, one of the busiest camping weekends. I tell myself to relax and stop worrying about the future; so far everything has worked out.

Michigan's Upper Peninsula might have been rich in minerals, but Hiawatha National Forest disappoints me. I remember as a child hearing Henry Wadsworth Longfellow's poem of the Indian hero. He undoubtedly was Ojibwa, Algonquin or Ottawa, related tribes who lived along the Great Lakes. From Longfellow's poem, *Song of Hiawatha*, and the illustration in the children's book from which I first heard the poem, I imagined a forest like the Olympic Rain Forest of Washington or the California Redwoods. This national forest, however, at least from my vantage point driving the Mo, looks more like scrubland than forest, the trees stunted and sparse, nothing like Northwest forests.

They may not have impressive forests here, but lakes they know how to do. Almost the entire day—a good six or seven hours—I drive along the western and northern edges of Lake Michigan, covering less than one-fourth its perimeter.

I'm staying in St. Ignace on the Upper Peninsula, a town established in 1671 by the French Jesuit missionary and explorer Fr. Jacques Marquette who was sent to Quebec in 1666 to minister to the Native Americans. He traveled and ministered throughout the northern Great Lakes area. The Jesuits who first worked in these mission fields, unlike many Christian missionaries, believed the natives already had a relationship with God the Creator and that much of their culture was inherently good. Realizing the problems alcohol caused in the native society, they opposed the colonial government policy of using it for trade with the natives.

At the Museum of Ojibwa Culture I view Native American artifacts, learn about the Ojibwa and related tribes and the history of the Jesuits in this region. I also visit Fr. Marquette's grave on the grounds.

🔥🌺🔥

"Are you all alone?" The elderly woman getting into the carriage behind me for a tour of Mackinac Island is a stranger.

"Yup." I settle into the seat and look out at the scenery. If she's at all savvy she can probably tell from the closed look on my face that I am reluctant to discuss this. It is difficult enough to do these things without someone pointing my solitude out.

The carriage trip is part of a package tour. The drivers provide interesting information, history and folklore related to the island, which prohibits vehicles other than bicycles, horse-drawn carriages and golf carts. I love horses but these big Percherons are so odiferous it is hard to breathe at times.

Mackinac Island has many handsome old Victorian-style homes with beautiful gardens. The history of the island includes the French fur traders along with Fr. Marquette and the Jesuits. The fort on the island changed hands several times among the French, the British and the Americans and was the site of a battle in the War of 1812.

John Jacob Astor established his American Fur Company here in 1808 and was a leader in the fur trading industry, bringing in furs from all over Canada and the northern Midwest. He made a fortune in Mackinac but over-trapping caused the industry to decline about the time Michigan became a state.

A butterfly conservatory is included in the tour. I consider skipping it but end up spending more than an hour absorbing some of the natural beauty, the eye-popping designs of our Creator—in all sizes and a wide range of colors and designs. I am reminded of Sue Monk Kidd's *When the Heart Waits*. She compares her time "waiting for God" to being in a cocoon. None of us comes out of our cocoons exactly alike. We all have a unique and individual beauty and are deeply beloved.

I'm convinced that one of the best ways to worship God is by spending time appreciating and admiring the wonderful gifts found in nature, and being thankful for them. Walking with God in nature and drinking in the beauty of creation is a form of contemplative prayer.

After taking the ferry back to St. Ignace, I stop to buy a pasty for dinner. These meat pies, a regional specialty, are similar to a calzone with pastry folded in half over meat and vegetables and sealed. It is filled with chewy little pieces of beef, very small cubes of potato, shredded carrot and onion. Locals often eat them with gravy, and I can see why; this one is quite dry.

⁂

Tuesday morning, we continue south, crossing the Mackinac Bridge, a five-mile-long suspension toll bridge that connects the two points of Michigan. I drive south to Flint, then east towards St. Claire/Port Huron where I have reservations to spend the night. I am within an hour of Detroit but the challenge of driving by myself in a large city dissuades me from making the trip.

I am on the edge of Lake Erie and on the edge of the country. Tomorrow I cross into Ontario, Canada. I'm surprised that the roads in Ontario are farther south than the roads I drive in Portland.

While in Wisconsin I arranged to visit a friend in New York. Geri sang in the church choir with me before moving back to the Rochester area a year ago. Charlie and I will stay with her while we explore western New York State so my failure to make reservations for Labor Day isn't a problem after all. Geri is also a widow, and I look forward to visiting with her.

Once again thunderstorms have found me. I know the area needs rain, and I should be thankful for the wet blessings. As Thomas Merton suggested, I try to be thankful that God's will for me is storms: rain, wind, thunder and lightning. The storms feel a bit like God in their persistence. You can run but you can't hide. God will find you. Maybe the storms help me get into a dark-night place, help me find a contemplative spirit as they keep me close to the Mo.

⁂

Charlie and I leave Michigan and the United States the morning of August 29 and drive into Ontario, the most direct route to New York. We seem to be in another world.

"Wow, we're really racking up the miles quickly today," I observe. Charlie gives me his typical bemused expression in response. "Oh, wait. Never mind. They're kilometers, not miles."

I enjoy the puzzle of trying to convert miles per hour to kilometers per hour. When I was in Italy, my rental car was set up for kilometers so not as challenging. I'm thankful the road signs here are in English.

The roads are in excellent condition, some of the best I've driven, so it probably is making for a smoother, faster trip. The biggest problem is there are no rest stops so it's hard to find a place to pull over to give Charlie a little break. No rest stops, but every exit has signs for at least one golf course.

As usual, driving affords me plenty of thinking time. Lately my thoughts are often with God, who has joined Charlie in the role of confidant and gentle listener. Before leaving Port Huron I changed the music selection on my CD player and am enjoying music by John Denver and Mary Chapin Carpenter, among others. I listen closely to the words and realize how often God makes an appearance, even in popular music, at least to my listening ear.

Many are love songs: sad, joyful or confused songs. Listening to songs that declare undying love, I wonder if that isn't what we all are seeking: unconditional love. I remember how well loved I was by John. Though there are challenges and difficulties when people share their lives, I treasure and miss that love and long to find it again, though it seems a lot to expect, almost a miracle.

Short of that miracle, I am learning I can live a full life as a single woman. My journey is partly to sort this out. If I remind myself often enough of how very much God loves me—more than any human ever could—that might diminish the pain of being alone. It's also true that people can be lonely and alone with a life partner. But given my choice, I would prefer to find someone wonderful to share my life with. These mysteries will unfold in God's time and not mine.

My brief foreign travels over, I arrive at the Niagara Port of Entry. The direction signs are unclear, and I miss getting in the correct lane. I am flustered; I can't back up and move to another lane unless I unhook my car. I sit there, confused, for what seems long minutes until a Customs and Border Protection agent opens the lane I am headed for and waves me forward. The slots are narrow and tight, and I bump my passenger side mirror on one of the overhead lights. I'm slightly amazed they don't arrest me as a terrorist or anarchist or crazy woman. They are actually kind and helpful and I thank them profusely for the work they do protecting our borders.

I readjust my mirror and drive across the bridge into the U.S. again, getting my first breathtaking, if brief, glance at Niagara Falls.

Chapter 10
Surprised by Beauty

*Pursuing what you want to do and achieving your goal is not like
finding the burning bush or discovering a gold mine. There are
usually no epiphanies, no sudden reversals of fortune.
Fulfillment comes in fits and starts.*
~ Mary Morris

I am awestruck by the natural beauty of New York. My first
experience takes my breath away as I cross the Rainbow Bridge
back into the U.S. I confess that the Falls—there are actually two
separate sets, one on the Canadian and one on the American side—are
far more splendid than I imagined.

On the way to the RV park where I'll stay the next two nights, I
pass numerous small farms and vineyards gathered along the south
shore of Lake Ontario and the east side of Lake Erie.

This RV park provides the rare treat of WiFi in my Mo. I am more
organized and get more done if I don't have to go somewhere to access
the Internet. I am able to confirm campground reservations for the
coming weeks, schedule a meeting with an insurance adjuster to get
reimbursed for my inverter repairs and have mail forwarded to Geri's.

I'm planning to return to Portland for John's scholarship fundraiser.
I'll leave the Mo at a campground about 50 miles from Boston and
catch a train to Logan International Airport. I book a flight for Oct. 3
returning on Oct. 9 so I will only miss a week of fall color.

My biggest concern is what to do with Charlie. A Portland friend
originally from Massachusetts had suggested this spring that her
mother in Massachusetts might be able to take him for a few days. I
send Sue an email to follow up on that possibility.

To learn more about the falls, I have signed up for a tour. The seven
people on my tour include an Asian family and an Israeli couple on

their honeymoon whose 45-day visit will include Orlando, the Caribbean, California, Mexico and Hawaii.

The Northwest is full of gorgeous waterfalls but from smaller streams. Niagara is a result of two Great Lakes coming together: Lake Erie flowing into Lake Ontario as it heads down to the St. Lawrence Seaway. The falls carry water that flows through lakes Superior, Huron and Michigan. The roar of millions of gallons of water plunging nearly 200 feet and smacking down into the lake below is deafening.

Niagara is the second largest waterfall in the world (Victoria Falls being first). About 188 feet high, the two falls together span a width of nearly a mile. The falls were supposedly first seen by a European in the mid-1670s when one of those intrepid Jesuit missionary explorers, Fr. Louis Hennepin, followed the loud thunder to its source. Tourists visit from all over the world, and the area has been a popular honeymoon destination since the early 1800s.

Our guide tells us the first person to go over the falls in a barrel was a 62-year-old schoolteacher who did the stunt to try to earn money for her retirement. Falls lore states she took her cat with her, but other sources claim the cat was sent down the falls a few days earlier to test the barrel. When the cat survived, Annie Taylor stepped into the barrel herself and emerged with just a few scratches. The cat was later included in photos with her, so it wasn't clear if she actually took the cat with her. I hope not: The idea of going over the falls is crazy enough, but taking a cat with you?! No wonder she had scratches!

After the tour I stop at a produce stand to buy fresh corn, potatoes, peaches and a pot of flowers to remind me of my visit.

🌲 🌼 🌲

"Are those dogs twins?" a woman asks as Geri and I are walking Charlie and Teddy on the pier that juts out into Lake Ontario at a city park in Rochester.

"No, just friends," I reply. It's understandable that people might think they are brothers at first glance. Teddy and Charlie look so similar that I have already mixed them up a time or two, just seeing their backs. Teddy is Geri's golden retriever-Great Pyrenees mix. He's taller and broader than Charlie and weighs about 20 pounds more, but they are almost the same color and equally handsome.

They are becoming good buddies and willingly share each other's food and water. Charlie is social and gets along well with most dogs; he enjoys playing with them and being part of the pack, though he prefers people. Groomers, vets and others who work with him often compliment his sweet and loving nature.

After our walk Geri suggests we stop at Abbotts across from the park for frozen custard. As we lick our treats, we talk about dating.

Although she is several years older than I and has been a widow longer, Geri still struggles with being alone. Her husband died suddenly of a heart attack when he was 55, the same age that John died, leaving her with several young adult daughters, a small business to close up and other challenges.

"I just haven't met any single men my age I am interested in starting a relationship with, or who are interested in dating me," she confides. "I don't even know where or how to meet single men."

"Oh boy, I know! I've only dated a couple of guys." I tell her briefly about Lance and Troy. "Unless you count my email correspondence with Keith, which really doesn't count in my mind. And I've gone out on a couple of random dates, met a few guys for coffee, but it's really hard to find good quality men who are interested in a relationship with someone their own age."

"Well, at least you've gone on some dates. I haven't at all. It took awhile before I felt ready, but now it just seems impossible to find someone to even go out with."

I tell her about the online dating places I've tried, with very little success.

"The few men I've met were just not my type at all. Some have no social skills and can't hold a normal conversation. Either they talk the whole time about things that aren't of interest to me, like quantum physics, without letting me get a word in edgewise, or I can't get them to talk. I'm not sure which is worse.

"A friend told me it's like shopping," I continue as we walk. "You have to spend a lot of time trying on a number of relationships before you find one that fits right. Problem is, I've never liked shopping.

"And what's with these men with big pot bellies missing half their teeth who want women who look like models? I don't get it.

"Some women are willing to put up with tons of flaws just to have a man, especially if he's got money. I know women who just don't feel they are whole and complete unless they have a man in their lives. Not me. I'm picky and don't plan to settle, even if means I have to stay single the rest of my life."

"Who wants to take on a project at our age?" Geri asks in solidarity. "I'm better off alone than with some man who thinks he needs to tell me how to run my life."

"Amen, sister," I say. We move on to a more pleasant topic. Dogs.

"They're such great companions," I say. "They never talk back or break your heart. They never insist you change the channel on the TV so they can watch dog sled racing or ask you to bring them a beer. A treat, maybe, but not a beer."

We both laugh and decide to share what's left of our cones with Charlie and Teddy, who are thrilled to share our treats and company.

"They give so much love and expect so little back," I say as Charlie licks my fingers. "My life would be terribly lonely without this big guy."

"Teddy's a great companion," Geri says, reaching down to pat him on the head.

🌲🌿🌲

On Saturday we take Charlie and Teddy to Seneca Lake, one of the Finger Lakes, and to Watkins Glen, a state park with deep canyons and waterfalls. Dogs aren't allowed on the trail so we don't get to see much. Many of the places I have traveled since leaving Oregon are not particularly dog friendly, especially compared to Portland.

We discuss other places in New York I might enjoy seeing, and Geri and Teddy agree to join us for a few days of exploring. It will be fun to have a guide along and a treat for Charlie to have a buddy.

I am again torn between the desire for companionship and the need for solitude for my spiritual journey, but I also believe God can use all circumstances to speak to us.

Tuesday morning after the Labor Day weekend, Geri and I pack up the dogs and take back roads to a campground in the Catskill Mountains. Undoubtedly the New York Thruway would have been faster, but we have less traffic and get a close, personal view of the towns, villages and beautiful countryside. The terrain is hilly, covered with deciduous trees. It looks rounded, soft and graceful.

Teddy and Charlie get along well, behaving like gentlemen, until Teddy discovers Charlie's stuffed pheasant that squeaks. He starts playing with it, and that triggers a little aggression with them pushing each other, growling, snapping. We intervene, settle them down, and they forgive each other and move on, probably more easily than humans would. Dogs don't hold grudges.

Wednesday we squeeze them into the Saturn and set off to explore the Hudson River Valley, a region full of historical and cultural significance.

Our first stop is Historic Hyde Park and the Roosevelt estate at Springwood. We pose for pictures with the outdoor bronze sculpture of Franklin and Eleanor and visit their gravesites in the rose garden. We walk the grounds including Eleanor's home, Val-Kill, and Top Cottage, a small private haven for Franklin.

Earlier we had watched the movie *Warm Springs*, the story of Roosevelt's personal struggle with polio and the rehabilitation facility he established in Georgia for others affected with it. The Roosevelts were influential people who made incredible contributions to our country, individually and as a couple. They were distant cousins, Eleanor was the niece of Teddy Roosevelt, and their union appears to have been a consolidation of power rather than love-based.

Leaving Hyde Park, we continue south to Tarrytown attempting to find Washington Irving's home, Sunnyside, but are unable to find it or anyone who can direct us there. Our trip through the village of Sleepy Hollow appears to be the closest we will get to Irving. It is also the closest I will get to New York City.

Though unplanned, we are on a bit of a literary tour as we drive through the Leatherstockings area and *Rip Van Winkle* territory. Last week visiting the Finger Lakes we were near Elmira, where Mark Twain spent most summers, wrote his *Adventures of Huckleberry Finn* and *The Adventures of Tom Sawyer,* and where he was buried.

We return to Rochester on the New York Thruway, and Geri helps me negotiate my first toll road from Kingston to Rochester. Mail I've been waiting for has arrived. I meet with my insurance adjuster and am relieved he can reimburse half the cost of the inverter. Tomorrow I head for New England.

"You drove that big thing all by yourself all the way from Oregon?" I smile and mentally pat myself on the back upon hearing this familiar question as I register at the Thousand Trails preserve in Sturbridge, Massachusetts, my next stop on the way to Maine.

The comment reminds me I am doing something outside the norm. Apparently people find it difficult to believe that a single woman in her 50s is capable of doing what everyone takes for granted when a man does it. It's nice to step outside the box and do the unexpected, help people open their minds to different paradigms.

However, my moments of smugness don't keep me from wishing I had a partner to share this journey. Driving past the exit for Cooperstown earlier reminded me that if John had been along, we would have stopped to visit the Baseball Hall of Fame.

Traveling the well-maintained toll roads is fast and convenient. Limited on- and off-ramps reduce my need to change lanes for oncoming traffic. Service areas every 20 or 30 miles have fueling stations with diesel and easy access for big rigs like mine, as well as places to fuel drivers on fast food and coffee. The speed and convenience come at a price, of course: $45 to drive from Rochester to Sturbridge.

I'm here primarily because it's on the way to Maine and has a Thousand Trails preserve where I can stay for free. I drive by Old

Sturbridge Village, but it seems very similar to Plymouth Plantation near Boston, which I visited years ago. I plan on returning to Massachusetts in a few weeks and spending more time so I take this time to just relax.

A large group of Latinos, part of a church group, is camping here. This interests me because I have seen very few people of color at the campgrounds. I write in my blog:

"This lifestyle of living and traveling in an RV seems to be an activity for middle-class, white, mostly older couples and families. I have seen very few African American families in the campgrounds. I have rarely, if ever, seen Latinos, or Asians or Muslims/Middle Easterners. Is this because they don't feel welcomed?"

Kristin, who works for Oregon State Parks, posts a comment: "OSPD did a survey on minorities and outdoor recreation, and they found that very few Latinos or Asians go camping at all. A decent percentage of the Latinos said they'd like to try camping, and the surveyors surmised that they probably don't go because it's one of those things you learn from your family, and if your family never went camping, you don't ever go as an adult, so it's a cultural thing." She added Oregon Parks was considering offering a class on "beginning camping."

🌲🌺🌲

Being alone after having a traveling companion again reminds me of my need for quiet time for prayer and reflection. I creep forward on my interior journey not knowing how long I'll walk this path or where I am heading. My road continues to be filled with potholes of negativity, fear and doubts. Maybe it's normal in the process of growing to experience days of dark questioning along with the forward movement towards light.

In an email exchange with my good friend, Marilyn, who is also one of my spiritual mentors, I share some of my misgivings and my confusion, especially regarding my interior journey.

"I'm not sure how much good I'm doing spiritually. But, hey, I'm trying; that counts, right?"

Her response is comforting: "I suspect that much is being done in you spiritually; that this may not so much be the time for 'doing,' but for allowing God to do and be in you. That kind of spiritual growth can often only be seen in hindsight—in the present it tends to feel like darkness, unsureness, the struggle to stay in the present. I have great confidence in your journey, your ability to discern, and that God is with you on this trip, but can also imagine the many challenges of it."

Having read the writings of the mystics and modern saints like Thomas Merton and Mother Teresa of Calcutta, it's comforting to remember they, too, had many dark days. Even Jesus, God-made-human, the night before his crucifixion, showed great anguish about the struggles he faced and begged God to spare him: "take this cup of suffering from me! Yet not what I want, but what you want." (Matt. 26:39)

I know this is how I should pray, and I try; if only I had the courage and trust to actually mean it. If only I could allow myself the refuge of knowing God's will for me is an easy burden, and that God will help me bear it. In a moment of surrender, I pray for the faith to trust, for the courage to turn my future over to God.

I know I'm nowhere close to being a saint, but I, like many people, am truly trying to do God's will and fulfill my purpose in life. Part of finding the fulfillment is getting past the days of confusion and learning to trust and believe in yourself and God, learning to live each day and each moment as fully as possible without worrying too much about what comes next or what happened in the past. All these lessons, steps and missteps lead to a destination we may not even know we are steering towards.

Chapter 11
Looking Deeper

*Your vision will become clear only when you
can look into your own heart. Who looks
outside, dreams; who looks inside, awakens.*
~ Carl Jung

"Hey, I like your choice in reading material," says the man as he and the woman with him sit next to me at the bar.

I pick up the book I have brought, *Teresa of Avila: Selections from the Interior Castle*.

"Not exactly what you'd expect to find in a bar, is it?" I smile. "I'm not used to eating alone in restaurants, and this is what I've been reading so I brought it along."

It turns out I didn't need a book; this is about my fifth conversation since I sat down at the bar in Mike's Clam Shack, a seafood restaurant in Wells, Maine. No tables were available at the restaurant or in the bar, so, summoning my courage, I took the empty bar stool.

I'm admitting my discomfort going to bars alone may have cost me some good conversations. I've already visited with two couples from New York State, a couple from Montreal and a man visiting from the Kenai Peninsula of Alaska.

Arthur, the bartender, recommended the lobster stew when I told him my mouth was watering for a taste of fresh Maine lobster. It is delicious: rich, creamy, buttery broth perfectly flavored, with chunks of lobster so big they are challenging to eat with just a spoon. I am sampling the haddock and scallops with chips when James and Margaret, as they introduce themselves, sit next to me.

The book provides a topic of mutual interest that leads to a lengthy conversation about my travels, travels in Italy and Ireland, their daughter who earned a PhD in theology at Boston College (a Jesuit school), and my children back in Oregon.

We cover topics on faith, religion and politics—all inappropriate subjects for polite company. When they learn that I am Catholic, they invite me to attend their parish church while I'm in the area. James recommends that I read the *Confessions of St. Augustine.*

They are surprised to learn that I had worked for 10 years for a Republican Senator and am still registered as a Republican.

"We might just have to change our views about Republicans after talking to you," James says. "If they're all like you, they're not as bad as we thought."

"Thanks, I think," I smile. "Republicans are just people like everyone else; some are more closed-minded or dogmatic than others. I've actually known some Democrats who are more conservative and closed-minded than I am."

"Touché," Margaret says, tipping her wineglass my way.

I enjoy this little lesson in judging people based on labels and am glad I may have helped them be more open to those who have a different perspective.

After finishing my meal I say my goodbyes and head home for a quiet evening under the wet Maine skies. I replay my conversation with the couple, thinking about political biases. I wonder if they would have sat next to me or struck up a conversation if they had known of my Republican affiliations. We have so many things in common that we would have never realized if we had been reluctant to talk openly to each other. I am saddened by political partisanship, not only among politicians but among citizens all over the country. We focus on one or two things we disagree on and ignore the numerous values we share.

🌲🌼🌲

"Dang, this is frustrating!" I say to Charlie. We have just driven to another beach and seen more signs prohibiting dogs. He looks at me with expectation and then disappointment when I don't take him onto the beach. "I'm sorry," I say, squatting down and hugging him. "I'm not sure why dogs aren't allowed on the beaches here. I'm sure it has nothing to do with you. We'll just keep looking until we find you a place where you can run on the beach." We spend much of the next few days looking for just such a beach.

When we first arrived at our campground here on the southern Maine coast, we went to nearby Moody Beach. Charlie and I both walked briefly in the Atlantic and wandered along the beach. There were a few people out but no dogs; there are always dogs on Oregon beaches. As we were leaving the beach, I discovered a sign stating dogs are only allowed on the beach certain brief hours.

As often happens when life sends roadblocks, our search for dog-friendly beaches reaps unexpected rewards. I am spending more time exploring the coves, bays, beaches and small towns. In our quest, we explore much of the southern coast of Maine.

While wandering, we stumble upon the Portland Head Lighthouse, supposedly one of the most photographed lighthouses in the world. I, too, take plenty of photos of the tall white light tower and the adjacent red-roofed house perched on a rocky outcropping. The gorgeous sunshine enhances views of rocky coastline, sailboats floating on an ultramarine ocean, leaves variegated with gold and crimson, and white cumulous clouds skipping across the blue sky.

A plaque on the grounds states Henry Wadsworth Longfellow often walked from Portland to the lighthouse for inspiration and was thought to have written some of his poems here.

Charlie and I explore the area around Kennebunkport where a number of people stop to "talk to" Charlie or comment on him. Dogs seems to be more highly esteemed here than in New York, in spite of the beach restrictions which perhaps protect shore bird habitat.

On the way to Kennebunkport we stop at the Rachel Carson National Wildlife Refuge. Carson, an early environmentalist, exposed the dangers DDT was posing to wildlife, particularly raptors. Her book, *Silent Spring*, led to a ban on DDT in the U.S. I remember her book particularly because my father owned a pesticide application business, and he considered her the anti-Christ. Now I am convinced she was an amazingly brave woman. It was difficult in the early 1960s for a woman to be taken seriously, especially if she had something radical to say. With apologies to my dad, and recognizing we don't have a malaria problem in Oregon, I will put up with a few mosquito bites to watch bald eagles, red-tailed hawks and other majestic birds soar across the sky.

We watch a couple of lobstermen loading up their traps. Fishing has been good, they say, but they are bringing their pots in for the season. We chat with three young girls (Megan, Mollie and Maureen, hinting at the Irish heritage common up here) and their mothers who stop to pet Charlie.

I should no longer be surprised at how friendly people can be if you have a dog and they love dogs. There's something about golden retrievers especially that invites petting and conversation with their owners. I'll be walking along with Charlie and some strange man will say something like "Hello, gorgeous!" I'm smart enough to know he's talking to Charlie.

Another day I enjoy a bowl of rich, creamy clam chowder on the dock in Cape Porpoise while watching an old lobsterman get into a little blue skiff and row out to his fishing boat. He wears a red shirt with dark red suspenders holding up his black pants. A baseball cap and big rubber boots complete his look. He maneuvers his skiff next to the larger boat, then clambers aboard, tying the skiff behind and idling off for another port or to check his lobster pots to see if dinner is waiting.

One evening after returning from our wanderings, we meet some new neighbors who arrived the day before. Jonathan is 8, has deep auburn hair and loves Charlie (once again Charlie has been the conversation-starter). Jonathan's mom is Deb. Dad is in Colorado right now for work but mostly works from home, which is their motor home. They are traveling the country and Jonathan is being home-schooled. What a great experience for him! He will get to see first hand places of significance in American history and get a great understanding of U.S. geography. The following night we visit over a cozy campfire and s'mores.

🌲🌿🌲

It has been raining off and on, soft days filled with drizzle and mists. Having lived in Western Oregon for 30 years, I am used to such days, but not in September, one of our loveliest months.

Tuesday there is nothing soft about the weather in Maine. It rains hard all day. I don my raincoat and take Charlie for a short stroll to the music of raindrops pattering on the leaves. Rain brings its own comforts. Walking in the woods, deep layers of dead and decayed leaves cushion my steps and mist in the treetops gives an ethereal, otherworldly feel. I appreciate the quiet here after the summer rush.

Every day I see more red and yellow amid all the green. The sumac and Virginia creeper are turning crimson. Occasionally I see an entire tree that has burst into crimson or scarlet or gold.

On our walk I find a few leaves lying in the roadway that are beginning their change in color. I pick up a maple leaf, half deep burgundy, the rest bright scarlet. I'm not sure where it was in the process—turning the darker or the lighter color—when it fell. Clearly it wasn't done changing when it was ripped from the tree that gave it birth. Maybe the wind and rain last night did the damage. I wonder if starting to change color before the rest of the leaves on the tree made it more vulnerable to the wind.

Reading excerpts from *The Interior Castle*, I reflect on beginning the process of change in spiritual growth, like the leaf, but not completing it, somehow getting distracted or interrupted. It seems sad to have the leaf not complete its full change, but at least it started and is already beautiful. I imagine God prizes whatever efforts we make to grow spiritually and enter more deeply into our souls.

As I chop carrots and onions for the chicken soup I am making, I wonder what causes some leaves to start changing color earlier than others. Is it better to be a lone leaf changing early, standing out in your beauty—but also being more susceptible to early loss, more likely to die before the rest of the leaves; or better to change with the majority of leaves, becoming part of a beautiful whole, not particularly noticed on your own but part of a larger picture than a single leaf can paint? I guess the leaves do what they are meant to do, whether they color early or on time or late. Maybe we also change at different times, when we are called to, if we are open to God's will, if we become what God imagines for us; and I think that can be quite different for each of us.

Aside from those necessary Charlie walks, I spend most of the day in the Mo. It gives me a good excuse to take a break from all the things I think I should be doing exteriorly while I am traveling our country. I fear I will miss something important, that I will waste this wonderful opportunity I have been given. But rain allows me to work on interior projects—not only in the Mo but inside myself.

On Thursday the sun reappears but brings along blustery winds. I had signed up for a cruise out of Kennebunkport but the water is too choppy so it has been cancelled.

My friend Sue calls to tell me her mother in Massachusetts has a medical condition that will prevent her from keeping Charlie for me in October. Yesterday I got an email stating the fundraiser has been postponed to early November so I cancel my airline tickets.

After all my thought and preparation, my plans have fallen apart. This is another reminder that I have so little control over life.

I need to start over figuring out how to return in November for the fundraiser. I consider just driving back in late October—depending on the weather—and that sounds appealing. I have been thinking about where I'll spend Thanksgiving and Christmas. I long to be with family and friends for those holidays. If I drive back, I won't have to worry about leaving Charlie. I can spend the winter in Oregon and renew my journey in the spring. It's not what I was planning but seems to make some sense. Maybe this is just God pushing me back towards home, at least for the time being.

I will be in Maine for another week or more, but instead of heading south down the Atlantic coast, I can start heading west across New Hampshire and Vermont. I want to visit Gettysburg so I'll veer south into Pennsylvania, then catch parts of Virginia and Kentucky before making my way home. I make campground reservations based on those new plans.

I feel some relief making plans for the next month or two. Having no certainty about where I'll be at any given time is a challenge for me. While it is nice to be spontaneous sometimes, I find it hard to be completely open-ended. This is probably telling me that I want structure and a little sense of control in my life.

🌲 🌸 🌲

Sunday morning, before leaving Wells, I attend Mass at St. Mary's, the parish James and Margaret attend. I don't see them, but before Mass I chat with the woman next to me, telling her I am from Oregon. She asks for my prayers for healing of a brain tumor. I give her a hug and tell her about my friend in Portland who's had surgery twice for a brain tumor and is now cancer-free.

"I'll see you here next time I'm in Maine," I say as we leave the church. I don't expect to be back, but I hope I've given her hope.

My new friends from Illinois, Jonathan, Deb and Tom (who has returned home) invite me to meet them for early lunch before I leave, so we head back to Mike's Clam Shack and one last visit over fish and chips.

After lunch, I put things away, unhook the Mo, hook up the Saturn, and Charlie and I head farther up and farther in, towards Lewiston and my date with Habitat for Humanity.

꧁꧂

Chapter 12
New Friends

We are all travelers in the wilderness of this
world and the best that we can find in our
travels is an honest friend.
~Robert Louis Stevenson

"Where the heck are we? Can this be right? This road sure doesn't look like it's going anywhere." Charlie looks equally puzzled as I pull over to check the directions Russ sent me in his latest email. This narrow, winding, unkempt road through the woods outside of Lewiston looks like it could end in disaster.

"Can there possibly be homes at the end of this? Have I taken a wrong turn somewhere? If I have to turn around, will there be a place with room to do that? Yikes! What have I gotten myself into? Again?"

I'm sure I've followed the directions correctly so I drive on, coming to a stop sign at the T in the road Russ mentioned. I turn left as directed, and we break out over a hill from which I see a main road. It could be the road to Russ and Carol's. "Aha, here it is!"

Russ and Carol Burbank will be my hosts for the next week as I volunteer for Habitat for Humanity Androscoggin County. Russ is on the Board; he and Carol have done builds through the national program, RV Care-A-Vanners.

Russ and I have been corresponding by email for a couple of months since I signed up for this build. He reads my blog religiously, often having some pithy comment to add. When I wrote praising the beauty of New York State, he cautioned me not to get too excited until I had seen Maine. I have been looking forward to meeting them.

After getting the Mo parked and leveled on their sloping lot, I introduce them to Charlie, and we get to know each other a little better. Carol is a retired teacher and Russ has many years of communications experience, including writing for the *Boston Globe* at one point. His comments and compliments on my writing have been encouraging and supportive.

Monday morning Carol and I drive over to the home that Habitat is building for a Somali refugee family. So many vocational education students are working there's nothing for us to do. We'll check back tomorrow. Carol is planning on my help with a fundraising golf tournament Habitat is holding Friday.

Our unexpected free day provides a chance to drive to Freeport, home of LL Bean, and a great opportunity to do some early Christmas shopping. On the way to Freeport, we drive by Casco Bay and stop to admire the amazing beauty of this rocky coastline with quiet bays and fjords. Maine's largest city, Portland, sits on the southern shore of Casco Bay.

"My Portland was named after this one," I tell Carol. "Two of its founders, Francis Pettygrove from Maine and Asa Lovejoy from Massachusetts, flipped a coin to decide whether to call it Portland or Boston.

"Hmmm, the Boston Trail Blazers basketball. Nope, don't like it at all," I reflect, thinking of Oregon's professional sports team.

Soaking in the beauty of Casco Bay, I strike up a conversation with an elderly couple and their son. They are from North Carolina and are on a cruise to see New England during the autumn colors.

Carol and I stop for lunch, and I sample a lobster roll—chunks of lobster on a hoagie bun, a local specialty. Seafood restaurants and drive-ins are scattered all along the highway.

This part of Maine seems a little wilder, a little less developed than the south coast. Russ and Carol's home is on a hill above No Name Pond (that is the honest-to-goodness name of it). I would call this a lake, but in Maine a pond is anything that is less than a certain depth, though no one I asked could tell me what that is. Behind their house are woods. Last night as Charlie and I were trying to sleep—actually Charlie wasn't having any problems—I heard the cry of either a loon or a wolf; both species are around here, (as well as moose but I don't think moose howl). This morning when I took Charlie on a walk in the woods I heard something stepping on branches. I kept watching for mad moose or wolves or other scary critters, but it was most likely squirrels or rabbits. My imagination made it seem more threatening.

Mid-September and it is already getting cold here—down to the mid-30s last night. Thank heavens I have a furnace. But one of the worries keeping me awake last night was whether I have enough propane to run the furnace all week. It will get very chilly if I run out. I might have to let Charlie sleep on the bed to keep me warm.

I finally spend a few hours helping with the Habitat house, measuring, cutting and then installing the top pieces of vinyl siding. In the afternoon I help Carol put together packets for Friday's fundraiser.

⁂

"Four years ago, I had a fairly normal life; I was a wife, a mother, held a full-time job. Then suddenly—in a matter of seconds and inches—everything changed, and I was no longer sure who I was or of my place in the world."

How do you succinctly explain to a group of strangers something you're not sure you fully understand yourself? I am speaking at the Wednesday evening gathering of the Court Street Baptist Church, Russ and Carol's American Baptist community. I'm trying to convey some idea of my journey—what I call my traveling retreat—and what I hope to accomplish: namely, to find new direction and purpose in my life.

I have joined them for a traditional New England boiled dinner: corned beef and root vegetables. (Do I HAVE to eat the turnips?) I am also on the menu, paying for my meal by giving them all something to chew on. Either I'm sounding somewhat intelligent or they're being very kind.

I'm never sure how people of other faiths will accept me, a Catholic widow, wandering around the country by myself. I should not have doubted these folks. Even though our dogma and services may be different, we share common beliefs that bind us together. We share a world view that is God-centered, a belief that loving each other, caring about each other in spite of differences, is at the heart of being the people we are called to be.

I recently read *The Celestine Prophesy* (James Redfield's 1993 novel) and am intrigued by some of the theories posed about "coincidences" (or synchronicity as Carl Jung called it). I am finding that concept borne out in my travels. I have had some interesting conversations this week with people about their lives, about my life and about things that we've learned as a result of people or experiences that have "fallen" unexpectedly into our lives. I am convinced God is working always in our lives to send us guides. We need to be open to listen to them and be willing to be guides for each other.

One woman relates a very touching and mystical story about an incident after her husband died 10 years earlier. He had told her to buy herself roses for her birthday if he died before her. On her first birthday after he passed away, she went to a florist shop to do as he had asked. A woman dressed in white handed her a bouquet of roses, saying they were from her husband. She asked the woman if she was an angel, and the woman replied "I'm your angel for today." She never saw the woman at that shop again.

In another conversation, an 87-year-old woman who had recently gotten a new pacemaker shares that she is a new woman with energy and enthusiasm. She believes it gave her a second chance at life, and she understands the importance of living each day fully. I think that is a valuable lesson for all of us.

🌲🌺🌲

Sunday morning I say good-bye to Russ and Carol, and head north and east. I have become very fond of them. They are a fun couple and seem to have a loving and supportive relationship.

I am spending the last days of September and of my stay in Maine visiting Bar Harbor and Acadia National Park. A friend and former co-worker who grew up in Maine and Upstate New York, Jason, encouraged me to visit Acadia in my travels to Maine.

This is the farthest east you can go in the U.S. It's not, however, as far north as many people assume. I am probably a good 50 miles south of Portland and some 200 miles south of Seattle, though the climate here is less mild than Western Oregon and Washington.

It seems the farther north in Maine I come, the more color I see. I envy the birds privileged to live in these trees and can't stop gazing and gasping at the variety of colors, everything in the spectrum from yellow through red. Imagine all the various shades from lemon yellow to gold to copper, and mauves, apricots, eye-popping reds, scarlets and burgundies. It's still a week or two from the best color, locals say. Perhaps God sends these gorgeous hot colors in the fall so folks who live here can carry that warmth with them into the cold, long winters.

After setting up housekeeping, Charlie and I explore Bar Harbor. Stately homes and inns share lovely views of the harbor and islands with tiny rental cottages. Cruise ships, including a tall sailing ship, and many smaller boats are docked or plying the waters.

Later I take Charlie back to the Mo and set off in search of a full lobster dinner. I've flirted with lobster in stew and a lobster roll; now I'm ready to make a commitment to the full meal. Maine has lobster pounds: informal places to buy lobster, fresh or cooked to go or to eat on site. Overcoming my reluctance to eat out alone, I find a lobster pound and my courage is richly rewarded.

The lobster is succulent and sweet (locals recommend cooking them in seawater for the best taste) but also very messy. The meat is in big chunks in the claws and tail but much harder to get at in the body section. Overall it's a bit easier to get than crabmeat. I would be hard pressed to say whether I like Dungeness crab or Maine lobster better.

Later Charlie and I drive to Acadia and up Cadillac Mountain to watch the sunset, doubting my willpower to get there early enough for sunrise. Looking west across the dark sable island, I see violet bays and straits beyond, backlit by glowing golden orange, reds and indigos with a brilliant fiery red and orange sky that continues to move and shift during the hour I'm on the mountain. I keep taking photos, unable to stop, hoping to capture a semblance of this magnificence.

Standing on Cadillac Mountain, I am surrounded by many couples sitting on the rocks, snuggling together in the cold wind. I think of John. If he had been with me, we would have been holding each other to stay warm. He would have been taking the photos. I think about my mom who would have loved this sunset. My thoughts make them feel present.

🌲🌿🌲

Charlie and I spend Monday morning exploring the rest of Acadia's scenic rocky shorelines and headlands. From several higher viewpoints I gaze down on Bar Harbor with its boats and cruise ships. I shoot numerous photos of the surrounding beauty.

I drop Charlie off at the Mo for a nap and drive into Bar Harbor for Internet access and to do a little shopping. I discover WiFi is available at some points in the city park so I find an empty bench. While I'm there, a man sits down on the other end of my bench. When I finish with my computer work, I strike up a conversation.

"So are you from around here or a visitor like me?" I ask.

"I'm visiting from Oregon," he says.

"No way! Where? I'm from Portland. Oregon, that is."

He tells me he's from Bend, a picturesque area of snow-capped volcanoes, sunshine and numerous golf courses in Central Oregon, about 150 miles east of Portland. We agree that Oregon's coastline is just as pretty as Maine's, but that we wouldn't mind coming back to this east side of the country again. He tells me he is heading back to Oregon today, which makes me homesick. I take heart in knowing that tomorrow I begin the first step of my journey back to Oregon.

Chapter 13
Living History

A journey is a person in itself; no two are alike.
And all plans, safeguards, policing, and coercion
are fruitless. We find that after years of struggle
that we do not take a trip; a trip takes us.
~John Steinbeck

oday has brought the most moving experience in my travels. The emotional impact of touring the Gettysburg National Military Park nearly equals my visit several years ago to the Vietnam Memorial in Washington, D.C. Vietnam was more emotional as it was my generation's war; I knew people who died in that conflict and found their names on the Memorial.

Gettysburg was the bloodiest battle in the Civil War (53,000 perished during the conflict). General Lee's first major defeat, it was the turning point for the Union Army. When the National Cemetery was dedicated here the following November, Abraham Lincoln's Gettysburg Address became one of the most recognized speeches in American history. President Lincoln was suffering from a mild case of smallpox when he wrote and gave the speech.

"We cannot dedicate, we cannot consecrate, we cannot hallow this ground. The brave men, living and dead, who struggled here have consecrated it far beyond our poor powers to add or detract..." Though I remember the words from grade school, I'd previously had no context, no true understanding of this battle or perhaps the entire Civil War. The significance of Lincoln's words can only be grasped after walking these hills and fields, baptized by blood and consecrated with the chrism of tears.

As I follow the paths on Little Round Top and Big Round Top, see the woods and ridges, Devil's Den and the Slaughter Pen where the battle played out, I feel as though I am walking on holy ground. It is eerie walking where so many had given their lives. As it seems all too often with war, I don't understand why. I don't see what the loss of all these lives—and this was just one battle—accomplished, except to keep the Union intact, and for that I am thankful. But why did it have to start in the first place? I am convinced that war is rarely the answer; if there are "just wars," they are very few and far between. I believe arrogance—the insistence on being right—greed and fear are the gods that demand we sacrifice so many of our young people.

Throughout the park markers indicate where various regiments were stationed during the battles. I am touched by the many memorials to battalions, regiments and brigades. Most indicate how many of their members fell during the three days, and some include the names of those who died. The monument honoring an Irish brigade from New York moves me deeply: the large bronze Celtic cross has an Irish wolfhound lying at its base, obviously mourning its master. Men from all walks of life died here: those whose roots went back 200 years and those who had recently immigrated, wealthy sons of planters, impoverished sharecroppers and factory workers.

Many who fought and died were men of deep faith and commitment, good men who might have accomplished much had they lived. Each believed they were on the side of right and God was on their side. God was probably in deep grief over the whole affair.

The lovely pastoral scenes—rolling hills, large oaks and maples flanking fields of corn—seem incongruous with the savage fighting that occurred here. At one point I hear melodic birdsong that seems like a lament being sung for the dead. Turkey vultures floating across the fields on thermals are a grim reminder of the blood that watered this land 144 years ago. I wonder how many of the trees had been here and witnessed the brutality. The boulders and rocks surely did.

Lincoln's brief speech admonishes us to never forget those who died fighting for what they believed in: state rights and the preservation of the Union. It is important to remember that even when we disagree, we have so many more things we agree on, freedom being chief among those values. I feel a deep appreciation for my country, knowing that we don't always get it right and sometimes screw it up terribly, but we are good people, with deep core values. And that is worth preserving. Maybe I can comprehend Lincoln's decision to fight the attempts of secession despite the incredibly high price paid on both sides, his efforts to ensure "that government of the people, by the people, for the people shall not perish from the earth."

"His name is Charlie. Would you like to pet him?" I squat down beside Charlie to be closer to the two children who are obviously admiring Charlie. They are like skittish little rabbits, ducking their heads and whispering their names shyly to me when I ask, as they slowly sidle up to Charlie and stretch out their hands. Charlie sits for them, raising his head up to them and giving them his gentle dog smile to encourage them.

We have encountered these Amish or Mennonite children helping their father sell produce at the Farmers Market in New Holland. I've sampled some delicious local cheese and bought some fresh apples, a small steak for me for dinner tonight and dog treats for Charlie.

After spending yesterday afternoon reviewing a painful piece of our country's history, this morning Charlie and I headed off to find living history in the Amish country around the city of Lancaster. We have driven through a number of small towns, like Bird-in-Hand, Smoketown, Intercourse, Providence, New Paradise, Blue Ball—some quite by accident as it's easy to get lost here. Many little farm markets and shops sell quilts, furniture, antiques and baked goods. I don't have a house and am not in the market for furniture or quilts, but I make the mistake of walking into a bakery in Bird-in-Hand. A cornucopia of delicious treats awaits: shoofly pie, homemade bread, pumpkin pie, carrot cake. I buy an individual pumpkin pie for my dinner and a small shoofly pie to freeze and take home for Thanksgiving.

Farms cover the rolling hills; big barns and silos dot the landscape. Horses pull black enclosed buggies past cell phone towers and massive John Deere combines. We are blessed with such diversity in this country, but also the gift of being able to live and let live, to allow people to follow their own stars, no matter how different they may look from ours.

Tomorrow morning we leave Pennsylvania, heading south for our next destination in Lynchburg, Virginia. I hope to explore the Blue Ridge Parkway then continue homeward through Lexington, Kentucky, and a visit with Kristin's friend Tina.

🌲🌼🌲

A funny thing happened on the way to Virginia. I was lying in bed last night when I received a clear realization that the immediate purpose for this traveling has been accomplished. I have trusted I will know when it is time to end the wandering, and I don't recall a time in my life when I've experienced a message this directly: It is time to head home. Lynchburg is south and east, the wrong direction. At 11:30 I got out of bed to look at my atlases and plot a different route.

Leaving Pennsylvania this morning I am still targeting Lexington so drive southwest into Maryland and then west towards West Virginia. But it seems even Kentucky is not on my immediate agenda. In western Maryland and West Virginia I encounter so many hills it becomes challenging to drive with all the downshifting. I should have expected hills: West Virginia is the Mountain State.

In the back of my mind, as I constantly shift up and down for the hills, is John's drive from Raleigh back to Oregon. The transmission went out in his rental truck in West Virginia, and he was stuck for two days in Charleston. I feel such a strong imperative to return home that this seems an unbearable delay so I head north for flatter ground.

The first night of my flight back home I find myself in Cambridge, Ohio. When I look over my calendar, I see so many changes of venue, multiple reservations crossed out; it is clear this trip has been directing me and not the other way around. This, more than anything else, reminds me I am not in control, and that is actually reassuring.

After eight hours of hard driving, I feel lucky to have found an RV park with electricity, water, sewer and WiFi in my motor home for less than any place I've stayed that isn't a membership campground. I feel a sense of comfort being in Ohio where my mother was born and raised. I visited here with her twice when I was young.

Tomorrow I will drive through Columbus and on to Indianapolis, skirting both cities as much as possible, then through Iowa and Nebraska. I pray the wind will be light because, if it blows, there is no refuge on those plains. I have no idea where I will stay tomorrow or why I feel so hell-bent on getting back to the Northwest so soon. I only know I have a strong sense that I need to go home.

🌲🌼🌲

"Hey there, do you need a man to drive that thing for you? I got a friend over here could probably get you unstuck."

I am sitting in a parking lot in Omaha, Nebraska, blocked by cars that have parked illegally in the fire lane, preventing me from making the turn to exit the parking lot.

"Gee, thanks for the offer. I'll pass. I seriously doubt any man could drive this thing better than I can." I flash him a sarcastic smile. "But if you can wave your magic wand, Princess, and get these cars to vanish from the driveway, that would help, 'cause no one could get through this."

He laughs and walks off to his car, clearly never intending to help, just being a smart alec.

This is supposed to be a relaxing little break in what has been three days of steady, hard driving across the Midwest. I left Des Moines this morning on the way to meet a friend for a steak lunch. Beth had returned to Omaha from Portland a few months before I started my travels.

It's almost required protocol when in Omaha to eat steak, especially if you can share the meal with a friend. I eat so many meals alone it is a treat to have company, regardless of the menu. The price I am paying for this steak dinner in frustration and lost time is higher than I would have preferred.

When I asked Beth to suggest a place, I stressed the importance of a large parking lot where I could park the rig without fear of getting stuck in a place where I can't turn around or get out. She assured me there would be plenty of room at the steakhouse she recommended.

I arrived and found an open area off in the back of the parking lot large enough to accommodate the Mo and the Saturn where they wouldn't block anyone else. We had a delicious steak lunch, said our goodbyes and went out to our cars.

As I approached the Mo, I saw vehicles blocking it. I let Charlie out for a brief walk while I assessed the situation. One or two of the pickups would have to be moved. I walked back into the restaurant and spoke to the manager who thought they belonged to men remodeling the store next door. I tracked down the owners who moved their pickups. I headed the Mo towards the exit, then realized I couldn't make the turn because of the cars in the fire lane.

So here I sit: my fear of getting stuck has come true. Not knowing what to do, I continue to sit until someone whose car I am now blocking needs to leave. Since I can't back the Mo up or go forward, I unhook the Saturn and move it, allowing him to escape.

After waiting another 10 or 15 minutes, the drivers of the two cars blocking me finally leave, and I move forward only to realize that the final turn to exit the parking lot is also blocked by illegally parked cars.

I'm ready to cry. I am angry and frustrated and just a little frightened that I might have to park here for the night, or at least until the entire lunch crowd leaves. It is well past 2, and I'm not sure when the lot will open up enough for me to leave.

Fortunately someone who is actually helpful and kind comes up.

"You look like you could use a little help. Is there anything I can do?"

"Thank you! Actually, I'm driving across the country looking for Good Samaritans. I did this on purpose to see if I could find a good soul to help me out. You are the first today; you win! Congratulations and thank you."

The humor provides enough of an emotional relief that I can think straight again. Since I've disconnected the Saturn, I can back the Mo up. I ask him to spot for me while I back between rows of parked cars a couple hundred feet or so. When I've gone far enough to jockey the Mo around, I wave my thanks again, then head back to where I had parked in the first place going the opposite direction. This gives me a straight shot out of the parking lot. I hook the Saturn up to tow, and, with relief, finally make my getaway.

One of my horrible nightmares has come to life: getting the Mo stuck. It wasn't as bad as I feared—fearful imagination always escalates predicaments—and, should it happen again, I will know how to get free. Disconnecting the car isn't my favorite chore, but it's not too difficult or odious (unless the weather is bad) and allows me to back up and maneuver. I have successfully overcome this fear.

🌲🌼🌲

Since leaving Pennsylvania, I've driven eight or nine hours a day, averaging about 400 miles, despite heavy windstorms and rain that make driving slow and difficult. This part of the trip has been a blur: driving to the point of exhaustion and crashing for the night when I find an RV park. I long for a capable partner to help me drive.

Charlie is also challenged by these long days; he doesn't sleep while I drive. When we park for the night, after a short walk, he curls up on the dashboard and is usually out for the night.

All this time behind the wheel, with Charlie often resting his head on my knee, gives me plenty of time to obsess about what I will do when I get back to the Northwest. I wonder if I have the heart to travel in the Mo again; there's still much country I haven't seen. My questions encourage me to accept uncertainty, to trust that things will work out, that what is supposed to happen will.

I reflect on some of the lessons I have learned on my travels: lessons about our country and myself, lessons about the goodness of people and the goodness of God. Was it a mistake to take the huge risk of leaving my job, selling everything? No, I had waited almost four years; it was time to make changes.

There have been many times when I questioned the value of this journey. There have been nights when I lay in bed feeling such loss and pain that I begged God to be with me. I pictured God lying beside me, holding me, comforting me while I wept tears of loneliness, anger, abandonment. There have been days when I wanted to throw up my hands in frustration. Facing struggles is part of the lesson, learning to turn my pain, loneliness and fear over to God, finding strength there.

I realize changes, challenges and lessons will part of my life, but I have learned by driving in heavy wind that if I hunker down and hold on to the wheel, eventually I will ride out the difficult times. I can get through anything if I have faith in myself and God.

It is interesting to look at my experiences the last few months and know that God has indeed been there so many times. But I don't think God says, "Sit back, darlin', and just let me take care of everything. Don't lift a finger." I think God helps by sending the Spirit of Inspiration, of Ideas, of Aha's! and sometimes the right people as guides or helpers.

I have often felt conspicuous in my aloneness, believing everyone else is part of a couple or group. Parents with children, elderly people with adult sons or daughters and grandchildren, couples—young and old. I worry people think I am alone because no one wants to be with me, because I am unlikable or difficult. It shouldn't matter what other people think. In truth, probably few even notice that I am alone; they're all admiring my handsome traveling companion Charlie. But reality isn't relevant when dealing with fears.

I also know I can survive difficult emotional challenges. I feel more alone these days than at any time since John's death. Kristin and Karl are both married; my retirement left me without daily companions at work. I am thousands of miles from family and friends facing challenges I didn't expect to be dealing with.

Although the parking lot debacle was the worst, it isn't the end. After leaving Omaha I drive into Iowa, heading for South Dakota and get lost looking for an RV park that doesn't seem to exist. In the midst of my wandering through cornfields, Karl calls to check on me because it is October 3, the fourth anniversary of John's accident and death. His thoughtfulness helps get me through a challenging and frustrating day.

Maybe this sense of being different is teaching me compassion for others who don't fit into our idea of normal, helping me understand and see the beauty, dignity and individuality in each of us and get past the limits and labels we place on ourselves and others.

If I keep my eyes open, messages and lessons are in everything I experience. Even the hard things—maybe especially the hard things—are important instruments of grace as I travel.

⚜

Chapter 14
Back Where I Began

No man can know where he is going
unless he knows exactly where he has
been and exactly how he arrived at his
present place.
~Maya Angelou

fter the beauty I experienced today, I understand why the Sioux
Nation fought to keep this land. The Black Hills country is a
mixture of pine forests, steeply rolling prairie land, amazing granite
spires and beautiful little lakes nestled in small valleys. I assume the
name "black hills" derives from the pine forests that cover the area.

Yesterday after arriving in Rapid City, I found a pet groomer and
made an appointment to take Charlie for a bath. He is getting quite
smelly. Since I've been taking my showers all along, I will spend the
day exploring alone.

I drive to Mount Rushmore and am awed not only by the beauty
and the overwhelming amount of work that went into creating it, but
by the patriotism and dedication that were behind it. The monument
was conceived, designed and sculpted by a Danish immigrant, Gutzon
Borglum, over the course of 14 years (with the help of about 400
workers and plenty of dynamite).

Borglum selected the four U.S. presidents depicted in the
monument—Washington, Jefferson, Lincoln and Theodore
Roosevelt—based on their contributions to the founding, expansion,
preservation and development of the U.S. The heads are about 60 feet
tall from chin to crown and the figures would be about 465 feet tall if
they were fully constructed and to scale. Borglum chose the granite
peak from which they were chiseled for its hardness, but also because
the southeast exposure results in the faces looking into the dawn: a
hopeful view of the promise each new day brings.

Visitors approaching the massive sculpture walk through the
Avenue of Flags. Flags of every state are mounted on columns listing

the year each state was inducted into the Union. I am surprised to learn that Delaware was the first state to join the Union.

Next I head for Custer State Park, which is equally impressive to me for its natural amenities. The road through the park is tortuous: 10 mph horseshoe bends, low clearances and tight S-curves. I drive the Saturn through tunnels chiseled into the granite that have barely enough room for one car at a time. The road threads through breathtaking granite spires appropriately named the Needles.

Abundant wildlife wandering or grazing throughout the park includes white-tailed deer, pronghorn antelope, wild turkeys, prairie dogs, bison and mountain goats. The park staff just completed the annual Buffalo Roundup (the misnomer "buffalo" persists, even here in South Dakota where they should know better) on Monday so most of the beasts are in the corrals for sorting, marking, and distribution either back to the park or to the auction house.

"You still might see some of the big, mean, nasty bulls that didn't have enough sense to come in off the range," one of the park volunteers tells me when I stop for information and a map. As I drive I see several.

Fall is at its peak, though the colors whisper here rather than shout boldly as in New England. Brilliant reds have been replaced by golden aspen, birch and willow, mixed with the dark green of the Ponderosa pines. It is equally beautiful though more understated.

I stop for lunch—a buffalo burger—before picking up Charlie, who smells much better. He is ecstatic to see me, and when I share the bite of buffalo burger I saved him, he forgives me for the bath.

🌲🌼🌲

I've appreciated a couple of easy days after my challenges in Omaha, but it's time to return to the road, and once again I am homeward bound. Leaving South Dakota, I drive into the northeast corner of Wyoming where the wind blows ferociously. The air it is blowing is frigid. There is no sun for solar heating; I can't get warm, even running the heater on high. I stop and put on warmer pants, my heavy ski socks and cowboy boots and a blanket over my lap.

As cold as it is, I am worried about weather complications, particularly snow. I stop at an information booth just inside Montana and ask the attendant for recommendations on the best routes—whether to just continue on 90 up to Billings or take a more scenic route.

"Boy, if I was you, I'd stay on I-90. We've got a winter storm warning and they're saying it's likely to snow in some of the higher places. At least on 90 you have other traffic, and they'll keep the roads pretty clear."

Holy Cow! Winter storm warnings on October 6? I'm glad I didn't wait any longer to come through the mountains! I push harder, running ahead of the storm and trying to beat winter. I run through rain in a few places, and the wind is constant. Snow covers the surrounding hills but the highway is clear. Eight hours and 438 miles later, I pull off in Columbus, 40 miles west of Billings. It's likely to freeze tonight so I just hook up the electricity.

The threat of snow is another reminder of John and his cross-country drive in the spring of 2003, which followed I-80 through Nebraska and Wyoming in late April. He ran into quite a bit of snow here. Many of the places I've been or experiences I've had these last couple months have brought John to mind, places he'd been, places he wanted to visit but never was able to, places his family came from. Perhaps this trip is for him and with him more than I realized when I set out.

Columbus is about 300 miles east of Missoula, and Missoula isn't far from the Idaho panhandle. Home feels much closer. But I have several mountain ranges to cross (including Bozeman Pass at 5,760 and Homestake at 6,375 feet) so I'm not sure how far I'll get tomorrow. I wonder why I am pressing myself, why I'm in such a hurry to get home. What is pulling me so urgently? I don't know where I'll stay or what I'll do when I get back. Maybe I simply miss friends and feel safer dealing with mystery when I know my way around and have friends and family close.

I don't like the stress of dealing with things like early winter storms and below-freezing temperatures while driving and living in a motor home. I consider selling it when I get back to Oregon. It feels too hard emotionally for me to continue this alone. It's been a great opportunity, and I've learned and grown a lot. But I couldn't really say it has been fun.

Uncharacteristically I listen to local radio stations hoping to hear weather forecasts. Most of the stations are country-Western and some of the songs are interesting: stories about heartbreak and cheating lovers, about pain and vengeance or the ecstasy of "true love."

It seems we've convinced ourselves that unless there is huge emotional upheaval, good or bad, it isn't "real" love. Many love stories lead us to believe true fulfillment is only found in the perfect other. The only perfect other, really, is God, the God we find at the core of our own being, the God we can only know by taking time to befriend and know ourselves. I consider the relationships I've had and question how healthy any were. Healthy relationships require both partners to be emotionally whole, and most of us don't even realize we're broken.

While I have regretted never feeling I was in love with John, aside from a few rough years, we had a successful marriage. We had common interests and beliefs, and we were a good team, supplementing and complementing each other's strengths and weaknesses. We were friends as well as lovers and enjoyed being together. I know we had a strong and deep love, and I miss him in my life, often longing to share with him something I am experiencing. But, at the same time, I know I need to move on to my new reality, to accept that I am alone, and there is a good likelihood that I may be alone the rest of my life. I need to find ways to be single but not lonely, to have good people in my life.

I think about looking for a job when I return to Oregon. Finding a job I would love seems almost more difficult than finding another life partner who fits. But a job is not a lifetime commitment, so if it provides companionship, purpose and a little income, it might be better to settle in that area than to settle for a man who isn't right.

🌲🌼🌲

I'm pushing hard through Montana this first Sunday of October, trying to avoid snow. I drive through a couple flurries early in the day, and it spooks me. Snow covers the hills and occasionally right next to the highway but none is sticking on the road. I make it past Bozeman, and then to Missoula.

The drive is filled with glorious visuals. Blue sky overhead frames a scene of sunlight sparkling on freshly fallen snow and dark evergreens wearing delicately crocheted wraps of glittering white. The Yellowstone River winds through valleys flanked by golden deciduous trees and deep green evergreens. Log homes perch on bluffs with smoke curling from chimneys. I am absolutely grinning from the beauty of it all.

I haven't found a place to stay so I drive over the mountains into Idaho. Like South Dakota, the trees here are in full color right now, mostly golds—willows, birches, aspens—but some brilliant reds and deep purples are scattered throughout. I have always thought the silver mining area around Kellogg is incredibly tortured and ugly. Today, the absence of evergreen forests allows the deciduous trees and shrubs to show off their brilliant colors, and the area is actually beautiful. How comforting to know that something humans have made so ugly can be brought back into beauty by our Creator.

I don't find a place to overnight in Idaho. With the change from Mountain to Pacific Time, I gain another hour so I keep traveling west. The threat of snow is gone but now home is beckoning, and I draw closer every hour.

Thinking about driving in rush hour traffic through Spokane in the morning, I push on a little farther. I have a membership campground in Moses Lake and call while stopped for diesel for the third time. There is no answer so I leave a message. A bit later I get a phone call.

"Yes, we have room for you to stay tonight," she tells me. "But you're lucky I got the message. We close the office at 4 on Sundays and I just happened to be here for another reason and decided to check the voicemails. When do you think you'll be here?" Once again it seems Fate or Someone has stepped in to take care of me.

"I'm just west of Spokane so maybe a couple hours?"

"I'll leave the information for the site on the bulletin board at the office and you can check in tomorrow morning. Drive safely," she tells me.

Feeling relieved that I have a place to park for the night, I head west, directly into the setting sun. I-90 is badly pitted and worn through this section, and the wind is strong and gusty; between the bad road, blinding sun, harsh wind and exhaustion, I fight to keep the Mo on the road. Eleven hours and 616 miles after leaving Columbus, I arrive at the park, hook up electricity and water and fall into bed, exhausted but relieved to be back in the Pacific Northwest, within a few hours of Portland.

🌲🌼🌲

"Hello, all! I am back in beautiful Oregon. I drove down from Yakima—where I spent a couple days with my mother-in-law—this afternoon and will be here for at least a week before doing some visiting in the Seattle area, and then back in Portland for a while. I have no clue what my next step will be, but for now I am just happy to be back."

This email sent to friends and family is my way of getting reconnected and back into my life. In many ways it feels like I'd never left, but I know my experiences on the road have changed me. I expect some of these changes will not be readily apparent to me, or perhaps to others. Over the next few weeks and months, it will take time to digest and distill some of the effects of this journey.

At the same time, I must decide what to do, where to live, whether to sell the Mo. I must decide if my odyssey is finished or only on hiatus for a time. I don't have to make these decisions immediately. I can just BE for a time, safe in the warm embrace of family, friends, my faith community.

I do know I am tired. Tired of traveling. Tired of being alone. Tired of driving continually, of being in places where I don't know my way around and everyone is a stranger. It is comforting to be with people who know your history.

Since I am pretty sure Troy is not the right person for me, we meet for dinner one night after I return.

"Troy," I begin, moving my salad around on my plate, "you're a great guy, and I have lots of fun with you. But I'm not in love with you. And I'm pretty sure you're not in love with me, either."

"Yeah, you're right." Troy lays his fork down and looks at me with a sigh. "I'm probably not in love with you, though you're very lovable." He smiles. "I think we'd be great together, we have so much in common. But we both married before when we weren't in love. Maybe you're right that we should hold out for that."

"So, just friends, then?"

"Sure. It's such a funny thing. A friend just introduced me to another woman last weekend. She was recently widowed. So now I can pursue that relationship."

"Good, I'm happy for you," I say, relieved it has gone so easily.

🌲🌼🌲

Later in October I spend a couple of days in Seattle reconnecting with family and friends. During this visit I arrange to drive to Tacoma and meet Keith, who has continued to read my blog and send me comments from time to time. Recently he told me his other relationship has ended. The potential I saw during our earlier communication is still there, and we spend time getting to know each other better, enjoying each other's company. We make plans to see each other when he comes to Cate's house for Thanksgiving.

In late October I write in my journal: Keith is so cute and sensitive and sweet. He seems so enthusiastic about everything. He makes me laugh and smile so often. He is delightful to be with and talk to and text message and email. I enjoy his company a lot. I want more of him. But is he a distraction to where I should be going?"

🌲🌼🌲

Back in Portland I talk with Fr. Peter about the journey and my future. He listens, asks a few questions and reminds me that God wants me to do what my heart longs for.

My heart continues to pull me to my parish, which has been integral in my life since we joined when Kristin was four. I've invested so much of myself here that I have a strong sense of ownership. Though neither was baptized at St. Ignatius, Kristin and Karl received all their other sacraments here and that is where we said goodbye to John. It has been my support, my stronghold, my safety for many years. I have learned so much and my faith has been nurtured and grown here.

Peter suggests I read the Annunciation from Luke's Gospel and take time to reflect and listen. Mary was "deeply troubled" when the Angel told her of God's plans for her. Isn't that the way with God's blessings sometimes? We hope to stay under God's radar so we don't get picked for a job we don't want, like students hiding to avoid being called on by the teacher when they aren't prepared.

I pray to figure out what my "work" is, what I am called to. Perhaps I am being called to more waiting, more solitude, more time to reflect and allow my experiences of this past year to steep or ferment in me.

But maybe I can do that waiting anywhere: Portland, Seattle, the Coast; in the Mo or a condo or apartment. Just a few verses later, the Angel Gabriel reminds me that nothing is impossible for God. God can take me where I am, with all my confusion and all my failures and mistakes but good intents, and make something useful from me, as long as I remain pliable and willing.

Then Peter reads Psalm 27: One thing I ask of the Lord; to live in the Lord's house all my life...and to ask for his guidance...Teach me, Lord, what you want me to do and lead me along a safe path...Trust in the Lord; have faith, do not despair." No answers, just more questions. But questions are good—they keep the conversation flowing and bring clarity out of misty, muddled confusion.

BOOK TWO

⁂

Chapter 15
Exploring New Paths

*Twenty years from now you will be more disappointed
by the things that you didn't do than by the ones you
did do...Sail away from the safe harbor. Catch the
trade winds in your sails. Explore. Dream. Discover.*
~ Mark Twain

"Why don't you come travel with me since you're not working right now. C'mon. It'd be fun. Imagine all the trouble we could find to get into. Just think about it."

I am verbally twisting Keith's arm. It's January and the rain is getting me down. I've been living in the Mo, parked most of the time in an RV park in Northeast Portland near the Columbia River. Last night lying in bed I had a sense of suffocation from the gray damp days, a sense of eternal sad grayness. I regret not being in the south as I had intended last spring.

The Mo is not built for winter living conditions, even mild western Oregon winters. When the cold air outside meets the large single-pane windows, they sweat. I continually wipe up water on the dash until I finally buy a dehumidifier, which pulls a gallon or so of water out of the air almost daily. I am also continually refilling my propane tank to keep the furnace running.

I have advertised my motor home for sale but without success. Is the Universe telling me my traveling days are not done? There are many places I haven't seen and would like to.

As I've watched the sailboats on the river, the jets coming and going from nearby Portland International Airport, and the Canada geese as they congregate for their southbound flights, I have felt pulled by a desire to see new sights and follow the sun. Shirley has reminded me how unfortunate it would be to quit traveling before I've seen the rest of the country.

Despite my desire to continue the journey, I'm reluctant to fly solo again. Watching the geese, I long for friends to travel with, companions to encourage me.

I don't need help but would love someone to share the experience with. If that someone can help drive, help me plan routes and venues, check maps as I'm driving and maybe chip in a few dollars for diesel, which seems to have dropped in price a little, even better.

Since meeting in late October, Keith and I have traveled between Tacoma and Portland several times and talked in between visits. There's an edgy side to Keith that didn't show up when we were corresponding. He's got some "bad boy" tendencies.

"You know, I wasn't real sure I even wanted to meet you," he tells me. "Cate's description of you made you sound like a saint or something. Normally I don't care for halos."

He has some of John's tendencies to be a bit of a rebel, push the envelope and challenge rules when he thinks they impede getting important things accomplished. He lost his dental practice by failing to follow certain requirements he felt were a waste of time. Now he's at risk of losing his license.

He can also be warm and caring, curious and intelligent, and has an offbeat sense of humor I appreciate. He and I don't have as much in common as I had with Troy, but he is a little less overwhelming. I enjoy his company enough that my invitation to travel with me comes despite some red flags. He seems very thin-skinned and easily insulted, doesn't have the self-confidence I admired and appreciated in both John and Troy. He is close to Cate, but not his two brothers.

Keith isn't as extroverted and sociable as John, Troy or Lance, and unlike them, he doesn't seem to have many friends. He has been married twice despite his efforts to make the marriages work.

When we first met, I was a little surprised to see he is only a couple inches taller than me and fine-boned. His lack of size may play a role in his sensitivity and defensive attitude.

Our views on a number of things, religion and politics for starters, aren't in sync, and he seems to view a number of things far differently than I do. Though raised as a Quaker, during one discussion he shared his doubts that Jesus was God's son.

"Wow, I think that's pretty non-negotiable if you're a Christian."

"So are you saying I'm not a Christian?" he challenged me. "I'm a Christian! What are you talking about?!"

I wasn't sure whether his doubt or his angry retort made me more uncomfortable. I'd seen this flash of temper before. I dislike conflict and avoid it as much as possible, though I enjoy lively, intelligent, civil conversations. Anger is an emotion I've never been comfortable with, but I've seen Keith exhibit it more often than I'd prefer, though rarely at me.

Undoubtedly he also sees things in me that he doesn't admire. I know I have plenty of room for improvement, though I'm coming to like, respect and appreciate the woman I am more and more. Even The Mother is coming around. Slowly. Perhaps my courage and ingenuity under fire, my competence and capability during the traveling have convinced her I have some acceptable qualities. Or I'm getting better at ignoring her negative sniping.

I am also wise enough to realize there are no perfect relationships, no partnerships that don't take a great deal of work on both sides. It's a matter of deciding if the good balances out the negative enough to make it worthwhile. There are enough positive things about Keith's and my relationship that I want to give it more time.

After traveling with Marian, Colleen, and Geri, I understand the many challenges of traveling with someone, living in such limited space. This would be for a significantly longer period of time and the added dimension of a romantic connection makes it more complicated.

By late January Keith catches my enthusiasm and agrees to join me. In a conversation we have before setting out, I broach the subject of finances, thinking it would be good to be upfront about what he's able to contribute towards food and expenses. He is unwilling to make a commitment or really even discuss the subject so I let it go. I am infatuated with him and enjoy our positive connection so am unwilling to make waves. It is typical of me to ignore my needs and concerns in order to keep the peace, though this is an unhealthy way to relate.

Having firmed up our departure date for February 8, I make reservations for our first two weeks in campgrounds in the Russian River Valley, near Santa Barbara, and east of San Diego.

Karl and his wife are expecting my first biological grandchild in July so I will return by then at the latest, though I tell Keith we'll most likely return in May. I realize everything can change overnight so avoid planning too far in advance.

A friend familiar with my writing background suggests I contact *The Oregonian* newspaper and offer to do some travel articles. I send an inquiry and pitch a proposal to the travel editor. Suddenly I have a commitment to do a series of articles and blog posts for Oregon's largest newspaper. This gives me even more motivation to move forward with this journey. I can't flake out now.

After sending my first article to the editor—a summary of the earlier travels and an introduction to the upcoming journey—his response brings me a smile:

"You know, I occasionally run into people whom it gives me the greatest pleasure to know. I am sure you are going to be one of those people. We will do some minor changes here, but if I told you how much I liked what you've written, you'd probably think I was exaggerating. I wouldn't be."

And so my journey continues, only now I will be sharing my journey and my story with even more people. Charlie and I spend an hour posing for photos for the first article that will be published the week I leave Portland.

🌲❀🌲

My brother Tom and I take Nick and Charlie on walks together as often as possible these last few days. They seem to know when they are going to see each other and get so excited, whining with anticipation. They clearly love each other. Further proof in my mind that not only are dogs intelligent but that they can love. Nick's health is failing, and we don't know if he'll survive till Charlie returns. He is a 13-year-old German shorthair pointer with congestive heart failure. I know Tom will be deeply crushed when he loses Nick. So will Charlie.

One of my last days before heading south, I meet a German woman at the RV park in Portland. Monika is spending a year traveling the U.S. with her two dogs in a small RV she bought on the East Coast. She has been to Alaska and many of the northern states and is heading for the Oregon Coast and then California.

During our conversation, I ask "If someone wanted to do something like this in Europe, is that possible? How hard would that be?"

"Oh, iss not hard," she responds. "I haff small motor home in Munich. But people in Europe think travelers like this are gypsies. They don't always treat them so nice.

"Motor homes in Europe are much smaller and the camping grounds don't have big enough spots for one like yours," she adds. "And, of course, the fuel is much more money."

We exchange contact information, and she promises to send me updates of her whereabouts and to read my blog when she can. I wish her luck, not knowing if I'll ever see her again.

🌲❀🌲

When departure day arrives, Keith is still waiting for tax forms. I decide to head out as planned; he will take the bus a few days later and meet me in Coos Bay. On Thursday, February 8, Charlie and I leave Portland.

I haven't driven the Mo for three months so have to get reacquainted with driving this 36-foot, 10-ton vehicle. I must remember to take curves more slowly or the Mo drifts and the load shifts. It also takes longer to start and stop.

Charlie immediately remembers his favorite place: sitting next to me, leaning on my leg or resting his chin on my right knee, close enough so I can rest my hand on his head or stroke his ears whenever the traffic, road and weather conditions allow me to hold the wheel with one hand.

The weather is spring-like: squalls of heavy rain and wind, followed by sun. This is the same route I took last May when I made my maiden voyage. Now I see standing water, creeks and rivers spilling over their banks. The Umpqua River is continually testing its banks and, in many places, winning the contest: covering the roots of the vegetation, leaving trunks and branches surrounded by water. Pale sage-green lichen hangs from the branches of the alder, oak and vine maple, mimicking early spring leaves and further contributing to the illusion that winter is over. In the pastures along the highway are more images of spring: new lambs exploring the world on shaky legs.

Charlie and I arrive in Coos Bay just before 5. Kristin and Ryan bring dinner: manicotti stuffed with spinach, basil, Italian sausage and cheese, along with salad, homemade Italian bread and a nice cabernet. Kristin never seemed interested in cooking when she lived at home, but she has become an accomplished and adventuresome cook.

Between spending time with Kristin and making final preparations, I have been reading *Eat, Pray, Love* by Elizabeth Gilbert. Kristin recommended the book, and I am struck by the things Gilbert and I share: a traumatic, difficult life marked with depression, anxiety and struggles, and the satisfaction of seeking your own heart.

I told a friend the other day that, in spite of missing John, I'm mostly happy with my life. A few years ago I was dealing with serious depression that threatened my safety and completely sucked all joy out of my life. I felt hopeless and broken and broke. I marvel at how much my life has changed, especially since I decided to retire, sell almost everything and reduce the clutter and responsibilities in my life. Freedom is a good thing and comes in surprising packages, just as slavery sneaks up on us if we're not careful.

🌲 ✿ 🌲

For nine months I have woken in the morning as the goddess of all I survey: pretty much my whole house since I can see most of it from my bed. That is about to end since tomorrow I will be sharing my tiny abode with another person. Even loneliness—my biggest challenge lately—appears resolved.

On my last morning alone, the Duchess decides to have coffee in bed, to act the part of the spoiled, decadent queen of the realm of Mo, to luxuriate in my aloneness. Having coffee in bed is easy since my bed is four steps from my kitchen.

Later as I'm hooking up the sewer with a new sewer-hose I purchased after my old one sprang a leak, I raise up from a crouching position too soon, hitting my head on the corner of the slide-out that extends a couple feet beyond the main part of the Mo. Excruciating pain explodes through my head. I realize I hit hard enough to break the skin and am bleeding from a cut in the crown of my head.

After sopping up the blood and putting ice on the wound, I take Charlie for a walk. No sooner do I let him run off-leash than he finds a dead sea bird to roll in. The stench is intolerable so I try to give him a quick bath in my shower. He is uncooperative, soaking me and the entire bathroom.

Earlier this morning, in addition to the dead-bird-rolling incident and the head-trauma incident, I encountered an electrical incident. The GFCI outlet that controls the bathroom and kitchen outlets went out. It wouldn't "pop." Apparently I need to replace the outlet, which also controls two of the outlets in the bedroom so half my outlets and both TVs are dead. Perhaps I should have taken today as a warning. But I soldier on and find a replacement GFCI at the hardware store.

I plan to pick Keith up at the bus station, then we'll meet Kristin and Ryan for dinner. Mid-afternoon my phone rings. Keith is calling to say he made the wrong bus connection in Eugene. I'm not clear on how this occurred but offer to drive back to Eugene, if necessary, or Roseburg if he can get there, and pick him up.

In subsequent phone calls, he tells me he got off the wrong bus just south of Eugene and has gotten a ride back to Eugene in time to catch the right bus—one of those "unexpected angels" has rescued him. His cell phone battery is dying so he will see me at the expected time.

I arrive at the bus depot a few minutes before he's due and wait for nearly an hour. Our dinner reservations are for 7 and the bus finally pulls in at 6:45. While I drive to the restaurant, Keith explains that the bus suffered two mechanical breakdowns, causing the delay. Because his phone battery was dead, he couldn't let me know. The frustration and stress of the delay and having to hurry to the restaurant without giving him a chance to clean up starts our travels on the wrong foot.

Sunday morning we leave Coos Bay and head down 101. I drive the first leg but just south of Crescent City, since Keith wants to learn to drive the Mo, I turn the wheel over to him. I've never claimed to be a teacher, especially for driving, but I do my best to explain the operations of the Mo, telling him things I'd want to know if I were driving it for the first time.

"Just remember to take the corners much more slowly than you would in a car. And it takes a lot longer to stop. Here's the exhaust brake; you can use that to slow down without using the actual brake. Somehow the engine helps slow us down. Here's how to set the cruise control; it saves fuel, so I like to use it whenever I can."

As we approach a steep hill I suggest, "You may want to take it out of overdrive; this hill is pretty steep."

Then a few minutes later: "Okay, we're coming to some tight curves so you might want to downshift and use the engine to slow a little."

"Maybe I've never driven a motor home," he says, and I can tell from the tone of his voice he is a little irritated with me, "but I have driven a big U-haul across the country. I know how to drive."

"Well, okay. I was just trying to give you some pointers and make sure you were comfortable." Chagrined, I sit back in my seat and try to relax. He is learning on a challenging course: the twisting roads, steep hills and tight curves on 101 through the Redwoods. I don't want to get into an accident or have something happen to the vehicle or us but I bite my tongue, reluctant, once again, to stand firm and take care of my own needs.

After a couple of hours we take a break, and Keith gives me back the driver's seat.

We arrive at the same Russian River campground Colleen and I stayed at in July. I disconnect the car, showing him the routine, and then hook up the water and electric.

"Here's where I hang the Mo keys," I point to the key rack next to the door as we come back in to the Mo after getting set up. I am trying to acclimate him to where things are since he will be living here for the coming months. "And I hang the Saturn keys on this rack above. Then I always know where they are and can grab them quickly if I need to."

"Oh my God, why does it matter as long as I know where one set is? Maybe you should show me how to wipe my butt, too. You are the most uptight person I've ever met!"

Shocked, I walk outside, shaken but trying not to show it.

I drink in the tranquil Northern California night, gazing at a dazzling sky filled with glittering stars. I'm not sure what I've said or done that triggered the explosion with Keith, but I know we have many days ahead of us and, despite my own anger and hurt at being spoken to so abruptly, I'm willing to try to make peace. After a few minutes of soaking in the beauty, letting the cool and quiet of the night wash over me, I step back inside.

"Hey, why don't you come out and look at this," I say reaching out a hand of friendship. "The stars are gorgeous out here."

He accepts my hand. We walk out to admire the night and the moment of anger passes.

It has been a long day, but I am concerned about what feels like his overreaction and sensitivity. I will try to accommodate his needs but am determined not to change who I am, minimize or discount what I have accomplished, my knowledge and capability, to appease him. I've done far too much appeasing in my life.

We spend the next few days exploring Northern California and visiting with Colleen and her husband Jeff. We drive to Mendocino to explore beaches filled with surfers and the eclectic mixture of expensive galleries and humble cafes where colorful earthy characters in tie-dyed cotton and dreadlocks meet over organic vegan food and fair-traded coffees.

Our route follows roads that are cave-dark from the huge canopy of redwoods overhead. Sun filters down through the trees, emphasizing their height and girth and beauty. We stop at Hendy Woods State Park to admire giant redwoods.

There is something deeply spiritual—mystical even—about the Giant Redwoods of Southern Oregon and Northern California. Tall and silent but embracing and generous, they offer gifts of peace, quiet and a prayerful presence. Some of these trees have been alive for millennia, since Rome ruled most of the known world and an itinerant preacher was nailed to a cross outside of Jerusalem. Imagine what these trees have witnessed in their time on earth.

Their roots go back beyond memory, beyond history, possibly before humans walked the earth. The Elders, we might call them. Wise enough to have withstood all that nature, beast and man could throw at them. There is a mystery surrounding them and one can't help but be awed by their size, their majesty and their age. For me, walking into a Giant Redwood grove is every bit as breathtaking an experience as walking into the Sistine Chapel. This is part of God's cathedral.

Another day we drive to San Francisco, visit Fisherman's Wharf, and enjoy fresh seafood as we sit along the bay gazing out at the water and soaking in the unexpected sun.

On the route home we stop at a couple of wineries in Napa Valley. The grapes that fuel the wine industry here are of ancient lineage. Their ancestors come from France, from Italy. Perhaps some of these roots came from vines that created the wine that same Jewish rabbi drank and preached about: I am the Vine, you are the branches. As a Catholic, I have deep respect for the fruit of the vine, which, at each Mass, we believe, becomes the blood of Christ. Besides, I happen to like a glass of good wine.

Our visit includes a long conversation with a tasting room host about politics, wine, and other issues. Typical of many Americans, he has liberal opinions on some things, conservative on others.

I ask about his views on immigration, and what others here think.

"My sense is, immigrants are welcome here if they are willing to integrate into society," he responds. "The problem is when immigrants—especially Asians and Latinos—come across as trying to create their own communities, not trying to be part of the society and culture they now live in. I think we're seeing that a lot and people resent it."

He believes people should not be able to immigrate unless they speak English. Coming from a moderately liberal man in his mid-30s who will support Barack Obama for President, this opinion is apparently held by more than just the politically conservative. I have heard it from other Californians with otherwise liberal political views.

This subject is of particular interest to me since I spent nearly all of my ten years as a Senator's aide dealing with the dysfunctional immigration system. The rewards of this work included being able to tell a young Russian that, since he had just become a U.S. citizen, he could petition for his wife and children to join him immediately. He left my office in tears of joy.

The challenges included explaining to a bright 19-year-old brought here as a toddler why he had no recourse. He cannot go to college, he cannot find legal work, and there is nothing under immigration law that allows him to become legal. He didn't choose to be here and is trapped by laws that don't work. Most people have opinions but no idea how complex and broken the current immigration system is.

We are enjoying sunshine and temperatures in the 70s, nicer than weather in Portland and Tacoma this time of year. Little golden buttercups dot the roadways, bright yellow Scotch broom blooms along the coastline, and pink blossoms cover the flowering cherries.

The first stop of our trip comes to an end. We have managed to smooth over our respective ruffled feathers and are enjoying each other's company. Charlie loves having two doting humans to pet him.

Tomorrow we head south, trying to avoid the traffic congestion around San Francisco. At some point Keith will probably take another turn at the wheel, and I will work to relax and not be too "helpful." I will try to trust, something that isn't always easy for me.

❧

Chapter 16
More Fruitful Steps

Every day you may make progress. Every step may
be fruitful. Yet there will stretch out before you an
ever-lengthening, ever-ascending, ever-improving
path. You know you will never get to the end of the
journey. But this, so far from discouraging, only
adds to the joy and glory of the climb.
~ Sir Winston Churchill

California is the state I have visited most outside of Washington, where I grew up, and Oregon, where I have lived for nearly 30 years. I am getting a completely different picture this trip.

This California reminds me of Ireland, a comparison I would never have considered on previous visits. It has been a wet winter; some areas that only received four inches of rain all of last year have already topped that in mid-February. The rolling hills and valleys are lush with a rich green, like vast bolts of luxurious, soft emerald silk loosened and draped generously over a well-endowed woman. Yet this lush grass will become a serious fire hazard as the rains stop and temperatures rise.

Leaving the Redwoods and vineyards, we follow 101 through the Sacramento River delta area, then on to the Salinas Valley. This broad, sweeping plain of fertility is enfolded by mountains and hills: the Galiban, Diablo and Coastal ranges, with the Santa Lucia range on the west to keep it from spilling out into the Pacific Ocean. It's as if the Salinas Valley is so big and important it takes all these mountains to hold it in check.

The Salinas Valley is called the Salad Bowl of the Nation for good reason. Growing up in the Yakima Valley in Central Washington and having lived for many years at the northernmost tip of the rich Willamette Valley, I appreciate fertile valleys. This one is miles wide and many miles long, with nearly every square foot in use.

Not only is the planting space-intensive, it is labor-intensive. Already in mid-February fields are well under production, and workers with hoes hack at weeds or carry and place irrigation pipe. Many of the men and women who work these fields, the vineyards, the orchards are immigrants and have fueled a debate as difficult and intense as the work they do. There is no shortage of opinions but, like many of our nation's challenges, there are no easy solutions.

John Steinbeck was reared in this country, and it forms the backdrop of many of his stories. In *Travels with Charley*, written in the 1960s when he was in his 50s, he wrote of how much the area had changed since his youth. I wonder what he would think 40 years later.

We follow 101 to our next destination near Santa Barbara. Russ and Carol have stayed at the campground east of Santa Barbara and highly recommended it. We plan to stay three nights.

The road into Rancho Oso is probably the most hazardous I've driven the Mo on. It winds through the Los Padres National Forest down towards the Santa Ynez River, around extremely tight hairpin turns over blind hills on a road so narrow it can only accommodate one large vehicle at a time. I am relieved when it opens to a river valley.

The ranch, nestled among rugged mountains, was once owned by a friend of Henry Ford. It was a favorite haunt of early film stars and artists working for the Flying A Studios in Santa Barbara.

We visit with a couple from Hillsboro, Oregon; they have just come down Highway 1, stopping at the Hearst Castle. When they hear we are heading to the Eastern Seaboard, they encourage us to visit the Biltmore Estate in Ashville, North Carolina.

To make sure we include things Keith wants to do, I have suggested we take turns planning outings. It is Keith's turn, and he wants to drive up the coast to Big Sur and the Hearst Castle. I am tempted to tell him this is backtracking; we were very close to Big Sur when we came through Salinas. However, a deal is a deal, and I don't want another argument, so we drive to Big Sur, but rather than touring Hearst Castle, we stop at the visitor's center and view it from a distance.

I am trying to be open and accommodating, although I confide to a couple of friends through emails that I am being so careful not to upset Keith again that I worry about losing myself and my focus. "I feel like I'm walking on eggshells," I write.

Being a pleaser who takes care of others, ignoring my own needs, is an unhealthy pattern. My conflict avoidance and fear of losing love can keep me from being authentic. I don't completely understand my discomfort with anger, except that when I was young my parents often yelled, slammed doors, and otherwise released stress in ways that must have felt threatening to me. I must have gotten the message that anger directed at me meant withdrawal of love. I have taken it to such an extreme that I take any negative feedback as personal and painful rejection. It is one of my challenges this year: speaking my own truth rather than what I think my listener wants to hear.

The Mother reminds me: "*Just because you are in a relationship now doesn't mean you can throw away the self-respect and self-confidence you've gained. You have worked too hard to get to this point of loving and taking care of yourself. If the strong and capable woman you are intimidates others—namely men—it is their problem, not yours! You need to stay true to that woman you have become. You cannot allow yourself to go back to allowing people to walk all over you, dismiss your wants and needs, put themselves and their needs ahead of yours.*"

I like how supportive she's becoming and nod in agreement.

"But there's no reason I can't compromise on some things and be a good hostess. We have a long road ahead of us, and neither of us can afford to be too self-centered."

"*Well, as long as you remember that and don't let his needs and wants take over. This IS your trip, after all, your journey of discovery. If you ask me, you've been mighty accommodating already just inviting him to join you without expecting him to really pay for anything. He's really just along for the ride.*

"*Accommodation is a slippery slope. Don't allow him or anyone else to commandeer your dreams. You need to fight for yourself, stand up to others, engage in conflict when necessary.*"

Even though I hate the thought of conflict, I agree I must take care of myself and make sure my needs are met. That is my job; no one else can or should do it for me. Nor should I try to do that for others, including Keith.

🌲🌸🌲

After our stay at Rancho Oso, we continue to San Diego. We have nearly a half tank of fuel, but I watch for diesel to fuel up as we approach the large metropolitan area surrounding Los Angeles. We finally see a sign advertising diesel in Ventura and follow the indicated direction to a station with diesel. It looks tight to get the Mo into and turns out to be very tight indeed.

We have to unhook the car to get the Mo close enough to the pump. After I spend $150 to top the tank, we reattach the car. Within three blocks we pass a station with wide spaces that would have easily accommodated the Mo without disconnecting the car. And the diesel is 10 cents a gallon less. It's a good metaphor for life: If you fill your life with things that aren't a good fit, you have no space when something better shows up just down the road. I think of this in the context of men: having my heart full of an old relationship that didn't work leaves no room for something newer and better.

I am thankful for Keith's help in unhooking the car, driving it out of the way, and guiding me in close to the diesel pump. His aid probably cut my time in half. I appreciate that and tell him so. I am hoping this is an example of the kind of teamwork we can look forward to.

⛀⚜⛀

I plan to meet a friend in San Diego. Donna had worked with me in Senator Smith's office in Portland. Before joining our staff, she had worked for years on Capitol Hill, including several years working for another U.S. Senator and for several federal agencies. She and her husband Dave moved to San Diego, and I look forward to reconnecting with her.

"Donna and Dave are fairly conservative Republicans," I tell Keith over dinner the night we arrive in our campground east of San Diego. "Donna's worked for a couple of senators and was a political appointee in D.C. Dave gives quite a lot of money to Republican candidates. I'm not sure how comfortable you will be with them, but we can avoid political subjects. I know they'd like to meet you."

"Why don't you just go without me?" he says. "They don't sound like people I'd want to spend time with."

I hope I haven't made him feel unwanted and regret saying anything to him, but the damage is done.

The following afternoon Keith and I take Charlie north to Oceanside to explore Mission San Luis Rey, founded in 1798 by the Franciscans. It is known as the King of the Missions and is the largest of the 21 California missions.

On the way back to the campground, we stop at a beach to let Charlie frolic in the sand. He is chasing me, carrying around the shoes I took off to run, and at one point drops my shoe in the surf. Keith takes photos of our frantic chase, me trying to rescue my shoes before Charlie loses them completely. It is only as we are getting back into the car that I notice the sign prohibiting dogs on the beaches here.

After returning home, while I fix dinner, I also mix myself a margarita; Keith declines my offer of a drink, choosing juice instead. We are having what seems like a very comfortable, compatible conversation. I get up to mix another drink and, for some reason, this upsets Keith.

"You have a problem."

"Huh?"

"You drink almost every night; I think you drink too much."

"Really? Two drinks is too much? I'm not sure why this is any of your business anyway. I never get drunk. I don't drink before I drive. And I don't have a problem."

I pour the drink I have just mixed down the drain. Then I grab the bottle of tequila and a bottle of vodka and pour them both down the drain. "There, do you still think I have a problem? Give me a break!" I storm into the bedroom. "And fix your own damn dinner."

Keith has told me some of his previous relationships have been marred by drug and alcohol abuse. He must assume I am just like these women. I hate that he judges me—what I do, what I say—based on his past relationships. He sees me through filters colored by those experiences. I am me, not them, and I don't like being compared to his previous spouses or partners. In spite of my earlier belief that we were a great match, I am now having doubts about the future of this relationship; we have been traveling barely a week and already have had two volatile encounters.

We keep our distance for the rest of the evening, being formal and cool when it is necessary to converse. The next day as he and Charlie drive me into San Diego to meet Donna, we continue to act like polite strangers. Since he has chosen not to join me in the visit, I have arranged to spend the night with Donna and Dave, giving us both a break.

🌲 🌵 🌲

San Diego is noted for its sameness of climate: sunny and warm. But at least half of my previous visits have occurred during unusual wet spells, and this trip continues the trend. I am beginning to think it's me. Donna and I have a pleasant, slightly damp walk along the waterfront and a good visit. I appreciate having a girlfriend to vent and share my doubts with.

The challenges with Keith remind me to be careful what I wish for. It's easy to view my life of solitude as torture, to convince myself I am lonely and need someone in my life. Now that I have that, I'm not so sure it's a good thing. I wonder if there isn't some kind of middle ground where I can have fun and pleasant companionship when I want it but without the hassles of a relationship. Oh, wait! Never mind; that would be what Charlie provides in my life.

The cooling-off period has been good for both of us, and we are ready to start over at least as friends, possibly as a couple down the road, though that is not certain. If I am honest with myself, I admit I have wondered if I drink more than I should. I tell myself a drink or two in the evening isn't anything to get too worried about.

Alcohol does add calories I don't need and isn't good for my health. I think it's habit more than need, and I don't think someone who has spent less than two weeks with me has the right to attempt an intervention. Regardless, it will be good practice for me to not drink around Keith.

In our attempt at just being friends, Keith openly shares with me how difficult it is for him knowing that I own the motor home, that I am paying for virtually everything, that I am clearly in charge.

"I feel like I'm just along for the ride," he confides, "and that's really difficult. I don't feel like a full partner in this trip. I'm afraid of you getting so angry with me that you kick me out. I feel like I'm walking on eggshells most of the time."

Until now it hasn't occurred to me that he might be having similar worries about upsetting me. I haven't considered how vulnerable he might feel with me seemingly holding all the cards, making most of the decisions.

"Well, I'm happy to have you contribute in whatever ways you want. I'd love to have you help pay for some of the fuel if you could. And maybe we can take turns paying for dinners or outings. Like tomorrow I can pay for the zoo and then next time you choose something, maybe you could pay. And I can show you how to help hook up to shore power, and you can drive whenever you want."

It is my turn to choose our next outing. Keith is not enthusiastic about the San Diego Zoo, but I have visited this zoo twice before with my family, and I think it is amazing. I have a deep appreciation for nature, for living things.

The animals and plants are fascinating, and the information provided about animals that are threatened and endangered—most because of loss of habitat—is a good reminder of the need to care for our earth and its creatures.

One of the things I like best about Keith is his quirky sense of humor, and what better place to be silly than the zoo. We have an enjoyable afternoon, taking lots of photos, goofing off. I buy a cute stuffed koala to take home for the grandchild I'm expecting in July.

🌲🌼🌲

It is raining the morning we leave San Diego so Keith suggests, rather than putting the vinyl "bra" over the Saturn and towing it, that he just follow me in the car. This seems reasonable. He enjoys driving but doesn't seem that comfortable driving the Mo.

"I think it would be good for me to have some time alone," he says. "You'd probably like that too. We may be spending too much time together, getting on each other's nerves. And you might actually get better mileage in the motor home if you're not towing the car."

"Sure, that's probably fine, though it will cost more for fuel. If you don't mind paying for some of the gas in the Saturn, go ahead and drive it."

Driving through rain over the Santa Rosa Mountains and through the Anza-Borrego Desert, the passes are wreathed in clouds. Rain runs down the edges of the highway in small torrents. In some places, visibility is down to a few hundred feet. Desert rain is not gentle.

We begin to see saguaro cactus, looking like huge deformed hands reaching up to the sky, as if they are trying to grasp the sun. We hope to spend some time around Tucson and visit Saguaro National Park before leaving Arizona.

In addition to the saguaro cactus, we see prickly pear, ocotillo, teddy bear cholla, as well as yucca, creosote, acacia, cypress and other desert plants. This is harsh country and only the sturdy and well-adjusted plants and animals can survive.

We drive through the Imperial Valley along Interstate 8 close to the U.S.-Mexico border and often see Border Patrol vehicles. We occasionally glimpse the fence that attempts, without much success, to keep undocumented aliens in Mexico. Keith, driving the Saturn, follows me through two Border Patrol checkpoints. A wicked little smile appears on my face as I think about telling them he is undocumented. Of course I would never do that; I know better than to lie to federal agents; that can only lead to more trouble than I need. Still, even having such a thought is a strong clue I'm disappointed with our relationship and wondering if it was a mistake to invite him along.

Not only have we had some unpleasant exchanges, but being with him distracts me from doing my interior work. Rather, our encounters take me back to negative thoughts and beliefs I am trying to outgrow. Instead of exploring new ways to be free from old painful stories, I am getting caught up in them again, blaming myself for the problems that have surfaced between us, and feeling inadequate.

At a rest stop Keith buys some turquoise and lapis jewelry from an elderly Native American woman. I accept them as the peace offering they are apparently intended to be. I am trying to find positives, to not look for negative ulterior motives in things Keith says and does. I have always struggled with personalizing comments others make, taking things in the most negative way possible. What is it in me that makes me think people don't like me when there is plenty of proof that quite the opposite is true?

After about seven hours of driving, we stop in Gila Bend for the night. For less than $20 we have 50 amp electric, sewer and water.

There are few amenities but when you just need a place to park for the night, you don't need swimming pools, lodges, or picnic tables.

Our next destination is near Cottonwood, south of Sedona. We plan to stay for several nights, though plans have a way of changing.

My ultimate goal is to be in Jacksonville, Florida, for Holy Week and Easter. My dear friend Kathleen, who used to sing in the church choir with me, moved to Florida with her husband shortly after John died. I have seen her when she's returned to Oregon for visits but it will be good to visit her there. Easter is in March this year—about as early as it can be—but we have nearly a month to reach Florida.

The campground near Cottonwood, though in a lovely setting, turns out to less well equipped than the place we stayed in Gila Bend. We have no sewer hookup, only 30-amp electric, and there is no WiFi. It is nestled down along Oak Creek, which is running very full and fast after the recent rains. I am nervous, but Tom, the manager, assures me they will know in plenty of time if the creek is rising. There is evidence that it flooded recently; several sites were destroyed when floodwaters tore out the utilities, leaving gaping holes and piles of red mud.

This is one of the Audubon Society's "special places," with hundreds of bird varieties. I watch Western Bluebirds, a striking bright blue blur in flight, and along the creek I spot a ruby-throated hummingbird, deep green with glowing magenta throat. A swiftly moving jewel, it flits out over the creek and away. Even the tiniest of things show us the Creator's love of beauty. Giant sycamores, ghostly grey without their leaves, reach up into cerulean blue skies, their branches crowned with mistletoe like patches of pale green hair.

Everywhere we turn in this area we find striking beauty. The amazing red rock cliffs and monoliths of Sedona provide an embarrassment of riches for anyone with a camera. But cameras are frustratingly limited in capturing the color and texture, the sunlight dancing across the rock, the panoramic display. The art galleries are filled with attempts to capture nature's beauty. They are only pale reminders of what the human eye sees in nature.

Monday dawns bright and blue and gorgeous, and we explore the ancient Indian ruins at Tuzigoot National Monument, masonry stone pueblos built nearly a thousand years ago. On previous visits to Arizona, I have toured other Indian ruins. There is something moving and mystical about connecting with ancient peoples who lived here long before Europeans settlers came. I am intrigued that so much is left of their homes but so little is known about their culture and why they disappeared.

We are nine miles from Sedona and make several trips to use the library for Internet access, to shop and to admire and photograph the beautiful red rock formations, many of which have names. Sedona was recently voted the most beautiful place in America by readers of *USA Today Weekend*. It is breathtaking, awe-inspiring, especially with snow on the upper mesas under blue sky and bright sunshine.

I first saw Sedona 27 years ago when Kristin was not quite 2. John, Kristin, and I flew with my mother to Tucson to visit my maternal grandparents. We rented a car and drove to Flagstaff and the Grand Canyon, via the Oak Creek Canyon and Sedona. We fell in love with this area. If only we'd have had the money to invest in property here. John and I were in Phoenix for a conference 11 years ago and rented a car to drive to Sedona for a night's stay. Being here reminds me of those earlier trips with my late husband and my late mother, a time when I still had a sense of security and love, an idea of my place in the world. This is a bittersweet stopover on my itinerary.

Sedona is an artist's Mecca, and we explore the shops and galleries at Tlaquepaque Village, a collection of 45 shops, galleries and restaurants. Sedona is also a center for spirituality, new age and psychic "arts." An entire wall of the information center contains brochures for vortex tours, labyrinths, retreat centers, meditation, holistic healing and treatment places, massage and reiki, among other offerings. It seems a perfect place for spiritual awakenings: the presence of a benevolent Creator is obvious among such beauty. It is bound to inspire creativity.

These days have rekindled my love for high desert country. The air is clear and fresh. The Coconino National Forest surrounding the city is desperately quiet. Only the occasional car passing through breaks the silence. I could live here—happily, I think. I love the adobe Southwestern, pueblo-style homes, the crisp air and sunshine. But it isn't home. Perhaps better to keep pictures of it in my mind—perfect and pure—than live here and become disenchanted. Like a long-distance love affair, I can savor wonderful encounters and memories without the daily challenges.

Everyone I've met here has been friendly; I wonder if they think they know me, they are so cordial and outgoing and helpful. How much of that positive reception, I wonder, is because of my expectations? If I am open and expect people to be friendly, maybe they are more so. Perhaps there's something special about this place: the smallness, its isolation, the beauty or maybe a special spirit that pervades it. Could be those metaphysical groups touting the vortexes and other natural phenomena have a point. Or maybe the seekers attracted to this place recognize me as one of them, a kindred spirit.

Our campground is a couple of miles from the turnoff to U.S. Sen. John McCain's Arizona ranch; we pass his driveway on our way to Sedona. Residents at the campground joke about how things would change in the "neighborhood" if he were elected President with all the Secret Service at the Desert White House.

While we are here, I call a mobile RV repairperson to look at that GFI plug that went out in Oregon. Keith had replaced it, but it still doesn't work. Apparently I'd gotten the wrong part. The repairman replaces the defective GFI so all my electrical outlets work again. I am pleased with the work and his reasonable charge.

One night we join some of the other residents of the RV park for a barbecue/potluck dinner. In spite of the negative first impression of the campground, we have come to love the place and its people. It is small—probably fewer than 30 sites—but warm and cozy and most of the people seem friendly and helpful, if a bit eccentric.

We sit across the table from a man and wife who tell us they travel from Idaho each winter. They share their impressions when they saw me drive in.

"Man we thought some little teenage girl was driving that big bus in. We couldn't believe it."

"Well, thanks, but I'm hardly a teenager." Apparently my long blond hair makes me look young from a distance. Over the years, as it has turned gray, I have lightened the color till now it is pale blond.

We visit with Jackie, an artist from Maryland via California who has been living in her motor home here for 3-1/2 months with a dog and two cats. She has artwork in galleries in Sedona and Jerome and plans to make this her base.

Dan, who organized the potluck and barbecue, once owned a deli and an ice cream shop in California and Laughlin, Nevada, but found he couldn't compete with the casinos there. Now he lives and works at the park and cooks the community meals, barbecues and breakfasts on the weekends. His Jimmy Buffet CDs play throughout the evening, reminding me to buy one before we get to Florida.

Most of the people I have met here are from someplace else. They came here for the beauty, the fresh air, the healthy, low-crime environment or to practice their art or craft. There are people here who travel south for the winter to avoid cold and snow, and others who leave Arizona every spring, traveling to the Pacific Northwest to escape the blazing summers. We have seen a number of vehicles from Oregon, Washington and Idaho in Arizona, many getting ready to head back home in the next few weeks.

After several days' stay we continue our travels eastward. Today we head for Benson, between Tombstone and Tucson. After that we will head southeast through New Mexico toward El Paso, Texas. I've never been east of Tucson in the southern part of the country, so once again I find myself entering land that is a mystery to me. The security of familiarity vies with the sense of adventure and hope of finding the next wonderful place. There is great challenge in letting go of the old to discover the new.

Chapter 17
Southwestern Twists and Turns

The road of life twists and turns and no two
directions are ever the same. Yet our lessons
come from the journey, not the destination.
~ Don Williams, Jr.

"Eeeyew! What is that?" I back away in disgust.

While petting Charlie the morning after arriving in Benson, I am appalled to discover he has picked up a stowaway, his own personal Cling-on. A fat, grey appendage about the size of a sunflower seed is hanging off his ear.

Quickly I get on line; I suspect it's some kind of tick. I've worried Charlie might get stuck with cactus thorns or attacked by spiders, snakes or scorpions; it never occurred to me to think about ticks. Obviously worry doesn't help. Most likely the tick attached when we let him run in some fields in Cottonwood. There is no grass or brush at this RV park, only rocks, gravel and cactus.

I'm not all that squeamish—okay, that's a lie—but there is something about a blood-sucking insect that really gives me the creeps. When my kids were small and playing Little League, they had their own baseball helmets so they wouldn't have to share with other kids who might have unwanted visitors in their hair. During head-lice incidents at their school, I checked compulsively for nits or anything that looked suspicious. Finding a flea in my house is enough to send me on a frantic cleaning frenzy.

Since I've never had to remove a tick, I also do a little research on the best way to do that. The information I find on-line conflicts with folklore: put a hot match on its end or cover it with petroleum jelly or oil to force it out. Instead, the directions recommend using sharp, pointed tweezers or tick tweezers to grasp the tick close to where it's attached, then pull it straight out without twisting.

The tick removal operation is where Keith exonerates himself, and I immediately forgive and forget all our previous conflicts. Holding Charlie still and trying to get hold of the tick with tweezers would have been impossible alone. I am able to hold Charlie while Keith grasps the tick with the tweezers.

After removing the tick, we drive to Tombstone to explore. We tour the cemetery with grave markers indicating who was shot or stabbed, who committed suicide, and the rare ones citing death from natural causes. They fought over anything with hair-trigger tempers and big guns. "Don't like the color of my shirt? So shoot me." The invitation was quickly accepted. Life was cheap. But I think if I had to live here I'd probably be drunk most of the time and looking for ways to shorten my lifespan too.

In Tombstone, however, I fall in love as I am walking past a shop with Charlie, window-shopping while Keith is in another shop. I am completely smitten with a beautiful silver and turquoise necklace. I walk on but then retrace my steps for a double take. When Keith rejoins me, I show it to him.

"Look at this? Isn't it gorgeous?!"

"Why don't you go in and look at it?" he suggests.

"Wow, I probably couldn't afford it. But it's so amazing!"

"Doesn't cost anything to look. Go check it out if you like it that much."

I am under no illusion that he is able, willing or even interested in buying something like this for me, but I give in to his pressure and hand him Charlie's leash. The clerk suggests I try it on. She encourages Keith to bring Charlie in to look. Charlie is suitably impressed. The Duchess thinks it's perfect.

The turquoise cabochon—nearly an inch-and-a-half by an inch and the color of deep tropical seas—is set amid large silver wings about six inches high that embrace my neck. Sharon Sandoval, a Navajo artist, created it and named it Pegasus, but to me the wings look more like flames, like the Phoenix or flames of the Holy Spirit at Pentecost.

There are many levels of meaning for me here: I am trying to be a Phoenix, rising from the ashes of my broken dreams. I am seeking the guidance of the Holy Spirit in this journey. Even Pegasus has meaning:

my flight from my old life to try to find a new one. Perhaps the Mo is my winged steed.

The price is far more than I've ever spent on jewelry for myself; in fact, it's more than anyone has ever spent on jewelry for me. This feels like a test: do I love myself enough to spend $800 on something that truly delights me? Am I worth it?

In the past I would have walked away, believing it was too much money for a piece of jewelry, then later regretted not buying it. I realize I will never have another chance to buy this piece of jewelry that has struck me so intensely. It is one of a kind, and I will never see this piece again. In spite of my parsimonious, practical Irish-Scottish heritage that tells me this is ridiculous, I pull out my VISA. The Duchess imperiously looks down her nose at me in the mirror and says *"Good for you!"*

"Well, that's what they make credit cards for," I say, justifying this extravagance to myself. "Now I'll have to figure out when and where to wear it. Maybe you'll have to take me out dancing when we get to Texas," I tell Keith.

In the afternoon we leave Charlie in the Mo and drive to the Saguaro National Park East, the Rincon Mountain side. The spring desert is green; winter rains have swollen the saguaro and they are fat and sassy. Unfortunately we're a few days early for the cactus bloom.

We drive the eight-mile Cactus Forest Drive, sharing the road with bicyclists, one walker, and several cottontail bunnies. We walk a short paved information trail and learn this is part of the vast Sonora Desert covering much of Southwestern Arizona, Southeastern California and a good part of Northern Mexico. It is ruggedly handsome country, austere and sharp. There is nothing soft, soothing or comforting about this landscape. Even the teddy bear chollo, soft and cuddly as it appears, is covered in nasty spines. But amidst the harshness is beauty. Fairy Duster wildflowers show off delicate, airy blooms of deep pink or purple.

It is Lent and seems appropriate to spend a little time in the desert. This place calls for an authentic life: there's no messing about in the desert; everything is purposeful and calls one to be present, pay attention, or risk being eaten by a cougar, bitten by a rattlesnake, stung by a scorpion or dying of thirst.

It is quite hot already, probably in the 80s, too warm to be in the car without the air conditioner running. Keith and I both get mild sunburns. Later this spring it will exceed 100° regularly until the summer rains come in July and August.

⁂

Early Saturday morning, March 1, we pull up stakes at the RV park in Benson. I'm surprised and pleased at how much more quickly setup and takedown go with a partner. While I scurry around getting the Mo set to travel, Keith walks Charlie, then helps me hook up the Saturn to tow for the first time since San Diego.

It will take two days of hard driving to travel the 800 or so miles to San Antonio so we share the driving. Keith drives the first segment and seems to be more comfortable behind the wheel. I make a conscious effort to not pay attention to what he's doing (or at least pay attention unobtrusively). I get up and walk back to the kitchen a couple of times, read my book and try to show I trust him.

Keith drives until we stop for diesel in Deming, New Mexico, where I take over. I am impressed with Las Cruces, seen from the freeway. It is nestled in the Mesilla Valley along the Rio Grande River with beautiful jagged peaks of the Organ Mountains on the east. The White Sands Missile Range and Fort Bliss Military Reservation are both nearby. Orchards and cultivated fields surround the city of about 76,000. This looks like a place I could live—especially with its 350 days of sunshine a year—and I'm sorry we didn't work time into our schedule to explore the city of "The Crosses."

We drive on, into Texas and El Paso. Now if you're thinkin' of that Marty Robbins song, "Down in the West Texas town of El Paso . . ." this is SO not that El Paso. It's a big city that nearly 640,000 people call home. Since it's right on the border, we don't get very far before going through another Border Patrol inspection point. They pull everyone off for inspection. It's like returning to the U.S. from Canada or Mexico through a border crossing.

As we are climbing a very long, steep hill, my engine warning light comes on. Although I'm not running the air conditioner, I am running the fan with the temperature set on cold. Driving up steep hills at 70 mph running the fan in 80-degree weather must have put too much stress on the engine. I turn the fan off on hills and drop the speed back, and it cools down to a more acceptable temperature. My poor Mo has been trustworthy, and I need to be more careful. I hope nothing is seriously wrong; fortunately we are near our destination for the night.

After 400 miles, we pull off at a little bump in the road called Van Horn. Charlie got thorns in his paws—Russian thistle or other burrs—when we stopped at the rest stop and information office outside of El Paso. The Van Horn RV park manager warns me the fenced-in dog run has burrs in the grass, so I put Charlie's leather booties on him before letting him loose. He is so cute, prancing around in his boots. Earlier I found a red Western bandana for his neck so he looks Texan. After his exercise, the booties are full of seeds and burrs. I am relieved to be moving beyond the desert country, which hasn't been very hospitable to Charlie.

※ ❀ ※

"This is beautiful," I exclaim to Keith. We are walking Charlie along the River Walk that winds through the heart of San Antonio. "I love the way they've incorporated the river, made it such a vibrant, integral part of the city! But the river isn't all that impressive, is it?"

"Yeah, for Texas you'd expect something really big, wouldn't you?" he says.

The springs at the source of the San Antonio River are fairly close to downtown San Antonio in the limestone hills, so it's still a "baby" river. But what it lacks in size, it more than makes up for in elegance, charm, fun and fiesta spirit. I think about the difference attitude can make and wonder if putting a more positive spin on my life would make it better. Perhaps I could learn to ignore Keith's angry outbursts and just let him vent rather than taking them personally and allowing them to make me feel smaller. Perhaps just telling myself I am lonely, that I need a life partner, is what makes me feel disappointed and sad. If I can stop focusing on what I am missing, I could free up my energy for enjoying what I have and celebrating who I am.

We wander through tropical plants, waterfalls and pools that create a feeling of paradise found. River taxis ply the waters both directions, with the captain serving a dual role as tour guide pointing out highlights.

"This is so cool! It reminds me a little of Venice, except the waterway is much smaller and no one is speaking Italian," I say as we wander past a mariachi band beckoning visitors to eat at one of the many outdoor restaurants overlooking the river. "I'm starting to get hungry; how about you?"

"Yeah, let's see if we can find some place to get some lunch. What do we do with Charlie?"

"Let's look for a place with outdoor seating."

We find a restaurant that allows Charlie to join us on the veranda. The menu includes a hamburger called Charlie's burger so of course we have to order one for him, along with our own lunches. The prices are reasonable and the food delicious.

As we continue along the walkway after lunch, we get amused looks from people and comments about what a handsome dog Charlie is. He keeps trying to drink the water out of the river and fountains. Because he is the only dog on the River Walk, I wonder if dogs are allowed; but I haven't seen any signs prohibiting dogs, he doesn't cause any problems, and no one arrests us or even gives us dirty looks, so it must be fine. Again, I seem to be worrying for no reason.

Before our walk, Keith and I visited the Alamo, leaving Charlie in the car parked in the shade. Had I realized this was originally one of the Franciscan missions—Mision San Antonio de Valero—established in the early 1700s, I might not have been so surprised at how small it is, tucked away among newer, much larger buildings.

It is primary day in Texas. Bill Clinton is reportedly in San Antonio stumping for Hillary, and we have seen media people and a small group of Obama supporters. Most of the conversations we overhear are about sports, not politics. Perhaps the Texans don't feel they have a dog in this fight.

🌲🌵🌲

We are camping along Medina Lake in the Texas Hill Country, about 40 miles from San Antonio. Bandera, just up the road, is nicknamed the "Cowboy Capital of the World." The weather is a balmy 70 degrees with clear skies overlooking rolling hills covered with ranchettes and estates. An article I read calls it one of the most popular retirement areas in the country next to Florida. It is affordable and close to both San Antonio and Austin. I suspect summers here are hot and humid, being so close to the Gulf.

After returning to the campground following an outing, we walk down to the lake and Charlie goes wading. He needed to cool off after bolting from the car to chase the deer out of his "yard." The deer are almost as thick as the trees and seem quite tame. They flip their large white tails at Charlie as he watches them from the dashboard, like coy maidens waving their handkerchiefs at hapless males. It's no wonder that, when he gets a chance, he takes off after them. In addition to the deer, Charlie seems fascinated by huge jackrabbits that hop away from him on long legs at dusk. Squirrels and feral cats wander through the campsites, and unfamiliar birds sing exotic melodies.

🌲🌟🌲

It is easy to drive through a region, look at the geography, visit the cities, sample some of the food, talk with a few people and come away with a completely inadequate understanding of the area. I know I am often guilty of this in my travels, sometimes not even stopping to visit the cities and sample the food. Digging below the surface gives a much truer picture of the country I call home.

The diversity of cultures throughout this country stems from the many people who lived and died here. The Indigenous peoples gave way to the English in the Northeast, the Spanish in the South, and the French in the North and the Mississippi Delta area. Other Europeans, Africans, Asians and others soon followed these settlers.

The English often get credit for establishing a European presence and bringing modern civilization to this continent. But Spain colonized much of the Gulf Coast and the Southwest—earlier, in many cases, than the English up north. In the early 1700s Franciscan missionaries from New Spain developed missions throughout Texas and the Southwest, as the Jesuits were exploring and developing missions throughout the Great Lakes region.

In order to go beyond cattle, oil and cowboys to get a flavor of Texas, Keith and I visit the San Antonio Missions National Historical Park, a trip that contributes greatly to our understanding of what formed this region. We visit Mision San Juan, with its beautiful bell tower, and the Queen of Missions, Mision San Jose.

The native peoples living here in the early 18th century included several small hunting and gathering bands who followed the seasons and their food sources. Their way of life was threatened by European diseases and by the more aggressive Apache and Comanche tribes.

The Spanish missions offered safety and more reliable food sources. The tribe members developed skills in agriculture, irrigation, working with metals and using more advanced tools than stone, antler and bone. In exchange, they gave up the freedom to wander, their names, their gods, their language, their entire culture.

I ponder this history and wonder how often I have given up my independence, my authentic self, in exchange for what seemed like security and safety, for choices that fit others' expectations more than my own needs. Certainly I have seen that in my faith life when I have bowed to rules and strictures that have prevented me from doing what I thought was the best for me.

I wonder about that in the context of traveling with Keith. I believe my original, conscious intention when I invited Keith to join me on the journey was to have fun companionship. We seemed to get along well, and I enjoyed his company. At the same time, I was reluctant to travel alone again but felt I needed to continue the journey. Having Keith along would help relieve my loneliness. Perhaps he also added a measure of safety, support and made me feel more "normal." But did my desire to fit in, to have a companion, to be safer trap me in an uncomfortable situation that I was beginning to regret? Was it too late to change that? Had I let myself down by giving in to my fears and need to fit in, and giving up the solitude I need?

✻

Chapter 18
Troubles in the Bayou

Adversity is the first path to truth.
~ Lord Byron

"Oh damn! Where did he come from?" Keith has just spotted the flashing lights on the police car coming up behind us.

We are driving on a four-lane divided highway around 60 mph. There were no speed-limit signs when it changed from a narrow two-lane undivided highway full of ruts a mile or so back, but Keith assumed it was 55 or 60. Apparently the speed limit didn't increase when the road improved.

"Looks like we found one of them thar speed traps them folks in Texas warned us about," I say in my best imitation of a Southern drawl, hoping to lighten the situation a little. To his credit, Keith seems to be taking it all calmly. We had been told that the police in Louisiana like to ticket out-of-state-licensed cars, knowing the drivers won't stick around to protest the ticket. It looks like the town of Woodworth will profit from our mistake.

The officer hands us the ticket, with a $200 fine that must be paid within the next seven days unless we want to go to court and fight it. Since we will be in Florida in a week, court is out. This ticket definitely puts a damper on what was supposed to be a fun excursion.

We had left our trailer park—in the most pejorative use of that term—near Kinder with Charlie loaded in the back of the Saturn, heading north to visit Natchez, Mississippi. I had been doing laundry on this Sunday morning—I am not sure if the clothes actually got cleaner or dirtier; it was that kind of place—and catching up on my trip research. I hadn't consulted the book my co-workers had given me when I retired, *1000 Places to See Before You Die,* lately and was curious what it might say about the Gulf Coast states. Other than New Orleans, there was nothing for Louisiana, nothing for Alabama, but the book highly recommended Natchez. I checked the map, and it looked doable. After pulling things out of the drier, I suggested to Keith that we check it out. It seemed a better option than hanging around the dumpy RV park.

Natchez turns out to be much farther than I realized. It takes about 3-1/2 hours to get there—not counting the delay in getting the ticket. We drive past corn and cotton fields and the outskirts of Alexandria before heading more easterly and crossing the Mississippi River into Natchez.

Natchez is the oldest civilized settlement on the Mississippi River and at one time was the fourth wealthiest city in America. Cotton and sugarcane were raised on huge plantations and made many planters wealthy. Hundreds of beautiful old antebellum mansions dot the city and surrounding area. We time our visit perfectly to catch the annual Spring Pilgrimage, which starts in March and runs through mid-April and includes tours of many of these Historical Register homes.

We decide not to pay for a tour but wander around downtown on foot, Charlie in tow, to look at a number of the homes, all built before the Civil War. At a couple of homes the owners are dressed in period costume, walking in their gardens with parasols and hoop skirts. We see stark contrasts, with mansions often right next door to unkempt little cabins looking like they haven't seen paint since they were built and appearing better suited for demolition than use as domiciles.

On our rounds of the streets to explore the homes, we visit briefly with others doing the same. We have seen the same two men several times, and finally I say hello and ask them how they are enjoying the tour. We learn they are from Ireland, have been in Atlanta for a conference but are visiting some of the old cities of the South to view the architecture.

"Oh I loved Ireland when I was there a couple years ago with my sister. Where are you from?"

"We're both from Dublin, well at least now. I grew up in Galway."

"We spent a couple days there, and in County Clare. In fact, half our time we were in the Western part. It was lovely and the people were so friendly! Then we spent about three days in Dublin, close to St. Stephen's Green."

Keith takes a couple steps away and turns as if he is done with this conversation, if he was ever even part of it. Saying goodbye to them, I stride to catch up with Keith who is walking back towards the car. As I near him, he crosses the street away from me, walking quickly, apparently to maintain distance from me.

"Don't we want to go down this street?" I point back to the way I thought we'd come.

"You can go whatever way you want. I'm going this way. I think I can figure out how to find the car on my own. I don't need you to tell me."

Following him, I wrack my brains to figure out what I've done to provoke his anger. Finally as we reach the car and load Charlie, I ask.

"Are you upset with me about something?"

"Yeah, you acted like I wasn't even there. Talking to those guys about your trip to Ireland. You just ignored me." He gets into the passenger side and slams the door.

"Well, you weren't in Ireland with me." I load Charlie into the back and get into the driver's seat. "I didn't even know you then. What was I supposed to do? Think up something to talk about so you could join in the conversation?" I start the engine and stomp on the accelerator to rev the engine before putting it in gear.

"You made me feel invisible. I hate when people do that!" He turns and looks out the window as we cross back over the Mississippi.

As I drive south we have heated words about our relationship.

At one point, overcome with anger and frustration I suggest: "Why don't you just find your own way home. Like, all the way back to Washington. Why don't I just pull over right here and let you out. You can go find a train or bus. I'm so damn tired of your moods!" I shout at him, slapping the steering wheel.

I am surprised at how easily I am provoked into anger by our disagreements. It is unusual for me to be so outspoken. I feel wrongly accused by things he says, like he doesn't know me at all and doesn't want to. He seems to get angry over ridiculous things and to see me as an unkind, scheming, selfish person.

"Well, fine, if that's what you want. I think it's pretty silly for you to get so upset with me and ruin this trip." He folds his arms and turns away to stare out the window again.

"ME? You think I'm being silly for being upset? You're the one who's acting like a child!" I am seething, but I resist the urge to pull over and kick him out. I resent that I am so furious with him that I would even consider doing that.

We don't speak for the next few miles. The quiet gives us both time to cool down and reconsider. I think about the commitment I made to take him along. Backing out now and abandoning him in the middle of Louisiana would be very unkind. Though it might feel good for a moment, it would be an irreversible act, and I would be miserable with guilt. I think of Cate. I don't want to disappoint her, at least. I am not an unkind person, regardless of what he seems to think sometimes, though I have a habit of being kind to others at my own expense. I am willing to try to patch things up and make the best of it.

We agree to continue the trip and try to stay friends. We make a pact to treat each other with a little more kindness, try to focus on the positives—and there are many—rather than looking for negative interpretations. We will try to respect each other and give each other more space and consideration, and see how things go.

As I drive south through Mississippi, past old plantations and cotton fields, including the home of Jefferson Davis, I am struck again by how difficult relationships can be and am unconvinced that I'm ready for that much challenge. My imagination creates a perfect partnership where there are no conflicts, but I know those don't exist. I need to become stronger and learn to appreciate and love myself more, to avoid getting so wounded and diminished by those inevitable hard times, before I enter into another committed relationship. I wonder if I'll ever be ready. Perhaps I am starting to see benefits in being single.

Nine hours after leaving the Mo, we return, physically and emotionally spent, falling into our beds, completely exhausted and hoping for a more positive day tomorrow. Thankfully, being this tired keeps me from lying awake replaying and analyzing our fight.

🌲🦋🌲

"Boy it feels good to be getting out of here," I say to Keith as we get ready to leave Shady Pines RV Park after two nights for our next destination. "This place has been just a tad uncomfortable for me."

"Yeah, finding the frog on the wall during my shower yesterday wasn't exactly the highlight of this trip," he agrees. Keith often showers in the facilities at the campgrounds. Showers in the Mo are cramped and necessarily brief because of a small water heater. He prefers the luxury of a long, leisurely hot shower. I prefer the convenience of having my shower close and knowing who used it last, so it is a good compromise for us both.

The few people we have seen here glare at us and seem unfriendly, almost hostile, and I feel like an unwanted intruder. The park is filled with travel trailers and a few singlewide mobile homes set on concrete blocks and tied down to rings in the ground, presumably to keep them from blowing over in hurricanes. Undoubtedly some are FEMA trailers installed when Hurricane Katrina left many homeless. We have seen many similar places in this part of Louisiana, along with unpainted shacks on concrete footings.

After leaving San Antonio and driving a long day through eastern Texas, including Houston, we were relieved to find any place at all to park for the night. Louisiana seemed none too friendly, and we found no room at the inn the first two places we stopped near Lake Charles.

But, perhaps sensing my frustration and exhaustion (sometimes whining helps), the ladies at the second place took the time to call a couple of other RV parks farther east and found us this funky little unkempt place. The proliferation of FEMA trailers in this area is probably why finding a place to park was difficult.

With hope for a better experience, we head to our next destination, less than an hour southwest of New Orleans. We plan to spend time in this French and Caribbean city tomorrow.

After setting up camp, we drive into Houma (pronounced Hoe´-ma) for groceries and a bank to get a cashier's check for the ticket. The Coastal Commerce Bank in Houma has incredibly friendly, helpful people on staff. They are so sympathetic when they hear about our ticket they don't charge the $10 fee for the check. Mary goes out to her car to get us a map of New Orleans. Then Nichole goes out to her car to get a set of beautiful Mardi Gras beads that they give me because we missed Mardi Gras, which they also celebrate in Houma. They suggest things to see in the area and go a long way towards making up for that small-town cop in Woodworth. Once again an unpleasant experience has led to positive outcomes.

We are in a part of the country far different from what I've experienced. Both the geography and the culture are stretching my comfort level. Keith and I are amused by the signs advertising "drive through daiquiris." Apparently it is legal to drive around with "frozen" alcoholic beverages, though the drivers are not supposed to drink them while driving.

Cypress swamps surround our next RV park. These huge old trees—that reportedly can live up to 600 years—rest with their wide feet planted in water. Their grey trunks have several buttress-like appendages—creating the wide span—as well as numerous "knees" (pneumatophores) that are extensions of the roots protruding above the water and allowing the tree roots to breathe. The trees are draped in Spanish moss that calls to mind scraggly gray beards spilling down off the branches, nearly reaching the fan-shaped ground palms that often grow beneath the trees.

The park has a large crawfish pond. We've seen a number of stands selling crawfish (or crawdads as we called them as kids growing up in central Washington). Down here they are crawfish, and you can buy them live or boiled ("bowled") at roadside stands or gas stations or just about anywhere. The locals raise them in ponds attended by hungry egrets. I've eaten crawfish before so I pass; I didn't enjoy them enough to repeat the experience.

I keep Charlie far away from the black water in the crawfish ponds and the creek that skirts the park. We are in alligator country, and they can move lightning-fast when they are after prey. I don't want Charlie close enough to tempt any of them. I haven't seen one yet, but I know they are in the bayous and swamps surrounding us.

🌲🦋🌲

Tuesday morning we drive into New Orleans—over the Huey P. Long Bridge, the first bridge to span the Mississippi River in Louisiana—to reconnoiter and decide what to do tomorrow. We were supposed to get thunder showers today, but it rained last night and early this morning and turns into a sunny, pleasant day.

When we take the Saturn exploring, Keith usually drives, and I commandeer the maps and navigate. It works out well for both of us since Keith doesn't particularly enjoy reading maps (except, of course, this means I am telling him what to do). In my earlier travels, trying to read a map while negotiating traffic in a strange city was daunting and dangerous, so I avoided exploring large cities on my own. In spite of our conflicts, today I am thankful Keith is along.

We drive through some beautiful areas: St. Charles Avenue, past Tulane and Loyola Universities, the Garden District and through the French Quarter, out to Lake Pontchartrain.

Along St. Charles, hundreds or thousands of people have thrown Mardi Gras beads into the trees and on the telephone wires overhead. Keith wants to score some "wild" beads from one of the low-hanging branches; he thinks it will make a better souvenir than buying tame, domestic beads at one of the many shops. This seems kind of a "male" thing, that desire to win a prize rather than buy it, the sense that biting into a freshly caught trout is better than eating fish and chips at Long John Silver's. I put on my Suzi Sunshine cheerleader face and try to be supportive as he retrieves several strings of faded beads.

Most areas we visit show few signs of hurricane or flood damage, but the closer we get to the lake the more obvious is the destruction. We drive through a marina where people are still clearing out mud and debris and doing reconstruction and renovation.

Keith is interested in viewing the Lower Ninth Ward. People have warned us against going into this area, but Keith is undeterred. I swallow my reservations and allow him to do a little exploring in the fringes of this neighborhood. More than two years after Katrina, the area looks like I imagine a combat zone would look.

Houses are boarded up and marked for demolition. Debris, dumpsters and piles of dried mud are everywhere. People sit on porches or loiter in the streets watching strangers with eyes both challenging and hopeless. These are the eyes we saw in the few people who ventured out during our stay at Shady Pines, a shell-shocked view of a world that has defeated them.

The next day we leave Charlie home and spend more time in the French Quarter, walking along the harbor, strolling through Jackson Square, past St. Louis King of France Cathedral—claimed to be the oldest Catholic cathedral in continual use in the U.S.—with its unusual triple spires.

The European roots of this city go back to the late 1600s when France originally colonized it. Spain took control in the 1760s, then, following two devastating fires that destroyed much of the city, ceded it back to France briefly in 1800 before Napoleon sold it to the U.S. as part of the Louisiana Purchase. Add to this mix the influence of Caribbean culture, and you end up with a spicy, colorful dish. Not only is the regional cuisine unique, but the jazz and Zydeco music were heavily influenced by Haitians and African Creoles.

After admiring the Cathedral and the horse-drawn carriages ready to provide tours, we wander into the French Quarter. I love the beautiful wrought iron balconies above funky little shops and restaurants. I find the Witchcraft and Magick shop intriguing, with its signs advertising spells, voodoo, gris gris, potions, spiritual advice and other mysterious products and services. (Marie Laveau was a famous Voodoo practitioner here more than 100 years ago; reportedly people still visit her grave seeking special favors.) We have lunch at a restaurant on Bourbon Street across from the Magick Shop so we can watch for anything exciting. Keith has gumbo and I have a shrimp po'boy sandwich.

A friend recommended we visit Jean LaFitte's Blacksmith Shop, now a bar named after the famous pirate who supposedly used the building—one of the few original French buildings left—as a front for some of his privateering activities. We pop in but it is the middle of the afternoon and fairly quiet. The dark atmosphere seems too brooding and intimidating for a sunny afternoon so we leave without sampling their Hurricanes, a popular local alcoholic beverage.

Keith seems reluctant to partake of the party atmosphere here, likely trying to protect me, maybe from myself. Evident throughout the French Quarter is a seamier side, and no one makes any attempts to cover up the tawdry reminders of debauchery. Before leaving the city, on the advice of the same friend, we stop at Café Du Monde to sample some of the delectable beignets, crisp, airy little fried French pastries.

There are so many things to see and experience in New Orleans that two days aren't enough, but there are other sites to see in Louisiana, so we bid adieu to this lovely French city on the Gulf Coast.

The next day, following the suggestions of the Coastal Commerce Bank ladies in Houma, we explore the very southern reaches of Lafourche Parish. We follow Bayou Lafourche south out of Houma down to Grand Isle. It feels as though we are traveling in a third world country. Poverty and the effects of numerous hurricanes have left this area battered, bruised, and mired in mud. Many places south of I-10 require travel over myriad bridges, causeways and roads that thread their way through swamps and over bayous.

We cross a long causeway to the resort area of Grand Isle, one of the barrier islands scattered along the Louisiana shore; one was supposedly the stronghold of Jean Lafitte. Grand Isle is also the small resort town on the island, home to about 1,500 inhabitants year-round, a number that swells in the summer to 20,000 or more.

Many empty foundations show where homes were before being destroyed by Hurricane Katrina in 2005, followed soon after by Hurricane Rita. Most buildings stand on pilings 10'-12' high. They are painted in mint green, butterscotch and lemon yellow, apple-blossom pink, coral and periwinkle blue.

We park at Grand Isle State Park and walk down to the beach, Charlie's and my first encounter with the Gulf of Mexico. The sand is soft and appears groomed. It is pale grey or tan, almost white, looking more like snow than sand. The water is much warmer than Oregon's beaches. In the distance we see the oilrigs, source of much of this region's economy.

We stop to find lunch at one of the few open businesses, a tackle shop and gas station. The choices are slim. In addition to some pre-packaged crackers, we end up with a small cup of boiled peanuts to sample. We have seen these advertised in numerous places, and we're curious but not ready to pay for a full serving in case we can't eat them. Turns out to be a wise decision. Raw unshelled peanuts are placed in a slow-cooker pot and simmered in salt water. The end product tastes much like a salty pinto bean to me, nothing like any peanut I've ever eaten before. They are considered a local comfort food; I prefer my peanuts roasted and crunchy or in peanut butter.

🌲🌼🌲

It is time to leave Louisiana—the most unusual of the states I have visited; fascinating but not particularly comforting to someone who grew up in desert country surrounded by mountains. It is already very humid—the air thick with moisture, like walking into a kitchen full of boiling pots with no exhaust fans.

I unhook the water, sewer and electric, close up the slides and let the engine warm up. I raise the hydraulic leveling jacks to retrieve the blocks and pads to stow them away and discover most are buried in mud. It rained heavily overnight, turning the dirt into a sticky mess. I don't have a shovel so use a stick to try to pry them out. They are completely stuck in the gumbo, not the seafood soup, but the slimy, slick, sticky mud that results when fine-grained silt becomes saturated. We can only rescue about half the blocks and pads; the rest are stuck.

After washing my muddy hands, I take the helm. Keith will drive the Saturn—we both still feel the need for alone time. I put the Mo in gear and release the brake but nothing happens. I give it more acceleration and still nothing. Obviously the blocks and pads aren't the only things stuck in the gumbo. I try rocking backwards and forwards, bit by bit, several times and finally, when I am about to give up, I give the accelerator an extra stomp and manage to break free. What would it have cost to get a tow truck to pull a motor home from the mud? I shudder to think and say a prayer of thanks we were able to get out.

From here we head into Mississippi, through the southernmost tip of Alabama and on towards Florida.

Chapter 19
Close to Paradise

Travel is fatal to prejudice, bigotry, and
narrow-mindedness.
~ Mark Twain

"Wow! I'm impressed!" I tell Keith after registering for a night at Florida's Suwannee River State Park in North Central Florida. "If this is what all their state parks are like, maybe we should be making reservations for those, especially at this price. It's only $16; that's less than almost any other place we've stayed besides my membership parks. And it's so nice, probably one of the nicest places I've stayed since I started traveling!"

The park has new comfortable and functional restrooms and shower buildings and full hookups. The sites are long and wide and easy to back into; several are paved for handicap access. It is a positive welcome for my first visit to Florida.

Throughout my travels I have bypassed public parks and campgrounds, assuming they are tent campgrounds that wouldn't accommodate my rig. If Florida's parks are representative, I've missed some wonderful places to spend my nights—and days.

This park is situated along the river made famous by Stephen Foster's song. Though Foster had never been to Florida or seen the river, his song became the official state song. The river begins in Georgia's Okeefenokee Swamp and makes its way through the Florida Panhandle to the Gulf. A park trail takes hikers to where the Withlacoochee River joins the Suwannee on its journey.

Keith agrees that the accommodations at this park are impressive. "I'm betting there are no frogs on the shower walls here. Wonder if they're all this great," he muses. "We might have to check out more after we finish our time at—what's the name of that place again?"

"You mean the fish camp? Something Italian—Pancetta or something—I don't remember exactly. That will be interesting." I'm referring to tomorrow's destination between Jacksonville and St. Augustine.

Our trip to Jacksonville will be primarily to visit with my friend, Kathleen. I will meet her for Holy Thursday and Good Friday services. When we sang together in choir, she stood next to me for the Triduum liturgies so this will be like comfort food, taking me back to the life I had before everything got turned upside down. She has a beautiful, soft voice that is wonderful to listen to, besides being a very beautiful person full of spunk, humor and kindness. I look forward to seeing her.

"I couldn't find much around Jacksonville for camping; Kathleen suggested this place. I've never heard of a 'fish camp' before. Wonder what it means. Sounds a little...fishy to me."

Keith is used to my offbeat sense of humor so he gives me a courtesy chuckle and a rejoinder. "Let's hope we catch a winner, a 10 on the scales, and it's a suitable fin-ish to our long drive," he jokes back.

This humorous give and take is one of the things I enjoy about having Keith along. We've had some great laughs that help compensate for our spats.

🌲🌺🌲

On our way to Florida, we spent two nights at an RV park in Alabama between Mobile and Pensacola, Fla. While there, I discussed life on the Gulf with a woman working in the office.

"Isn't it a little frightening and dangerous when the hurricanes come in?" I ask when I learn she has lived on the Gulf all her life.

"Actually, people here enjoy watching them," she said. "There's a kind of party atmosphere. You usually know several days ahead of time—unlike tornadoes—so you can board everything up. Usually you're pretty safe, but things can go wrong. We lost our home a little over three years ago—we were living near Pensacola then—when Hurricane Ivan came through. There was a much higher tidal surge than anyone expected. Our house was flooded and ruined. We've been living in our camper since then. What're ya gonna do? It's where I live and there's problems just about everywhere. Don't you guys have earthquakes and volcanoes out there on the West Coast?"

She's right; there are challenges no matter where you live. In addition to the possibility of earthquakes and volcanoes, we have been known to experience pretty intense windstorms in Oregon, not to mention cold, snow and ice in the winter that can be very hazardous, especially if you have to drive over the mountains. The Gulf area has its summer humidity; the Northwest can have gray, rainy winters when we wonder if we'll ever see the sun again. It's all a matter of which risks you're willing to accept and what you are accustomed to. Ultimately, it's the people—family and friends—who make a place home.

🌲🦋🌲

We arrived at our fish camp—a quirky little marina, RV park and fishing "resort" (definitely NOT a 10) along the St. Johns River—early on St. Patrick's Day. We're invited for an Irish dinner of corned beef and cabbage with soda bread with Kathleen and her husband Jim but have time to kill so we take a quick trip to scout out the coast.

St. Augustine is on the Atlantic side of Florida so we take our initial wade in the Atlantic Ocean (Maine's coastline was too rocky and the water too cold). I'm delighted to find more of the soft white sand and warm water we experienced along the Gulf, but this is an ocean beach, with breakers coming in and going out, like the ocean breathing. Dogs are allowed on leash at this beach so Charlie will join us next time.

Keith decides to stay with Charlie instead of joining us for dinner. Maybe he's shy or not comfortable being with people whom I've known and been close to for many years. We're here for a week so he will have other opportunities to meet them. I set off in the Saturn, knowing Charlie and Keith will take care of each other again.

🌲🦋🌲

Southeastern Florida is where the European colonization of our country started. Texas and California can brag about being big and powerful. Virginia and Massachusetts can be proud of their long history, but leave room at the top for Florida. In 1513 Juan Ponce de Leon, serving as the first governor of Puerto Rico (having traveled there with Columbus' second voyage), first landed on this continent. No one can prove if St. Brendan or the Vikings were actually here earlier so Ponce de Leon gets official credit.

He had heard stories of a place with water that supposedly prolonged life. There are questions about what, exactly, he was trying to bring new life to. Some historians suggest that if he'd had access to Viagra or Cialis, he would have stayed in Puerto Rico and never gone searching for that Fountain of Youth.

Ponce De Leon landed near St. Augustine on Easter Sunday, which is known as Pascua Florida, the Feast of Flowers, in Spain. Under this name he claimed this new land—and all the land attached to it—for Spain. Based on this claim, the entire North and South American continents were considered Spanish territory, at least by the Spaniards.

Ponce de Leon laid a cross of stones into the ground at the spring he believed was the Fountain of Youth after being guided to it by Native Americans. Fifty-two years later the first European city in the country was founded here in 1565—on the feast day of St. Augustine of Hippo —almost 50 years before the first English settlers landed at Jamestown or the Pilgrims came to Plymouth Rock.

Older than San Diego, the California missions or San Antonio, St. Augustine, the city of the Fountain of Youth, is the oldest city in the country. The archeological exhibit supposedly including the spring is a popular tourist attraction.

Keith and I take a group tour, and the information and entertaining stories by the guide introduce us to St. Augustine. The tour includes a sip of water from the Fountain of Youth and gives us enough background that we follow it up comfortably with several days of individual exploring.

Florida has had a variety of cultural influences, including Spanish, French and English, but St. Augustine strongly evokes the Spanish history. It has a city square, similar to that found in Mexican cities, with the Catholic church opening out to the public area and shops encircling it. The old fort—Castillo de San Marcos—sits on the edge of the Matanzas River, with the Atlantic Ocean visible in the distance.

🌲🌸🌲

While Keith, Charlie and I spend our days visiting the areas around St. Augustine and on the beaches enjoying the sunny weather, my evenings are spent at Holy Week services. As I sit through the Catholic services here, I know three hours later my friends in Portland will be doing many of the same rituals: washing the feet on Holy Thursday, venerating the Cross and reading the Passion of Christ on Good Friday, welcoming new Catholics into the community at the Saturday Easter Vigil, and celebrating the Risen Jesus on Easter morning. I feel closely tied to my faith community in Oregon.

I share my thoughts about Christians praying together this Holy Week with a friend back in Portland. She responds: "It's like a wave of prayers and rituals coming across the country." In truth they are coming across the world, because the West Coast and Hawaii are among the last places to celebrate Easter.

I like the comfort of feeling connected in any Catholic Church; no matter what language they use, I know what is happening and can participate. Some of the local customs might be different but, at its heart, the Mass is the same everywhere.

I have been thinking about Kristin and Karl this week. I love my kids so much and am so thankful for the gift they are to me. I reflect on this powerful love I feel for them. I want what is best for them. I want to do whatever I can to protect them from pain, to shield them from hurt. Over my nearly 28 years of motherhood, there have been times I placed myself in danger or jeopardy to protect them from harm. Even now that they are adults, I find it hard to let go, to learn to trust that they will be safe and well without my help.

I ponder the possibility that protecting our children can prevent them from experiencing painful lessons they need to grow and become whole, to reach their true potential. My need to try to control what onslaughts affect my son and daughter may have handicapped them. I need to let them fly on their own just as I need to learn to do.

This love I feel for Kristin and Karl gives me a sense of how much God loves each of us, but God's love is unlimited, beyond the human capacity to love. There is nothing I can do that will ever put me beyond God's love and forgiveness. Yet God did not step in to protect God's precious Son, Jesus, from experiencing horrible pain, humiliation and death. God did not throw up roadblocks to stop or forestall Jesus' suffering. Jesus needed to experience this passion and death to fulfill his role of being fully human, of dying and rising so we all might join him and his Father.

Rather than showing a lack of love or caring for Jesus, it shows how very much God loves each of us that God would allow Jesus to be sacrificed on our behalf. I think about the hard times in each of our lives. We may pray to be delivered from difficult challenges, but my own life has shown me how pain can lead to growth and wisdom.

God doesn't give us these trials, as some believe, but allows us to experience them, to move through them, knowing that God will be with us. God trusts us to be able to deal with suffering, to grow and become more whole through it. I know I have developed greater compassion for others. Perhaps it is only in losing someone we love dearly that we truly realize the depth of that love.

During this Holy Week as I have reflected on this great love God showed for all of us, I feel deep awe, humility, gratitude and trust. I am more inclined to turn my worries, my prayers, my cares, and my children over to God and allow God to make of them whatever God wills. The trust and faith to do that is part of what I seek as I travel across these many roads and places.

On a beautiful Easter morning, I am thankful for the challenges that brought me here at this time in my life. I remember other Easters spent with family members who are no longer on earth. Those memories continue to bring me joy, even as the loss continues to bring pain.

Easter in Florida is like a dream for those of us used to rainy, chilly Oregon Easters. The sun is shining as puffy clouds race across the sky, playing tic-tac-toe among the jet trails. No rain for the services, no rain on the Easter egg hunts, no rain anywhere this bright Easter morning. Somehow sunshine does a better job of conveying the hope and joy of Easter than rain and gray clouds.

Tomorrow we continue our explorations of Florida after being at the fish camp for a full week, the longest we've stayed in one spot since leaving Oregon. It has been a good rest and a wonderful visit, but there is still much of Florida left to see.

🌲🌸🌲

"Monika? Is that you?" As I finish registering for three nights at Jonathan Dickinson State Park near Hobe Sound, I hear the person behind me talking to the ranger. I whirl around. It is, indeed, Monika, the woman from Germany whom I met this winter in the RV Park in Portland.

"Oh my goodness," she says in response when she realizes it is me. "This is so unbelievable!" She has been sending me updates of her travels as well as reading my blog posts, and I knew she was making her way along the Gulf Coast after being in Mexico in December.

"Amazing!" I say, still slightly shocked at seeing her here, thousands of miles from the last time I saw her. "We're just arriving too. We've been up by Jacksonville. How long are you here?"

"Only for a night. Next I go north to Georgia and will finish by driving to New York where my friends are. My visa is ending, and the girls and I need to go back home," she says, referring to her two dogs.

"I need to go park now and let you get registered," I say, "but I'll try to find you after we get settled and maybe we can catch up. It was so good to see you!"

The campsites here are separated not by trees and brush but by Spanish bayonet. Aptly named, it is a very sharp-leaved plant from the Yucca family that looks like a type of palm, though its fronds are not soft and flexible, but stiff, sharp barbs.

Spanish bayonet is not the only flora that gives this park something of a desert feel. We see a number of prickly pear cacti, many in bloom. Despite my disappointment at being in the Sonora Desert too early, I didn't completely miss the cactus bloom after all. Maybe God is trying to show me that surprises and delights can be found anywhere and at any time, even the last place we expect to find them if we keep our eyes—and most importantly our hearts—open to them.

There are also swamps, and for the first time we are seeing signs warning of alligators. We haven't seen any yet but obviously they are in this area. During our visit with Kathleen and her family, her daughter talked about an alligator that had been sighted in one of the golf course ponds near her home. I have mixed feelings about seeing them; they are fierce but fascinating creatures that deserve respect and caution. I continue to keep Charlie well back from ponds and rivers.

We take the Saturn into Hobe Sound to pick up mail that was forwarded there and to explore. As we drive into town, we notice the road continues on across a bridge. After our errands at the Post Office, we follow the bridge and discover it leads to Jupiter Island. Huge gated estates line the roadways, and we are awed and curious about this beautiful place.

This small island of 650 residents includes some very wealthy people, including several very notable golfers (Tiger Woods, Gary Player, Nick Price) and a couple of famous entertainers (Celine Dion and Alan Jackson). According to my research, it has the highest per capita income of any place in the U.S.

Less than two weeks earlier we'd driven through desperate poverty in parts of Louisiana. This stark contrast emphasizes how unevenly material blessings are distributed, with the vast majority of Americans falling somewhere in the wide middle ground. It reminds me that the gifts of talent, perseverance and good luck that can lead to such wealth are exactly that: gifts generously given by a loving Creator.

Though many people put themselves or others on pedestals based on material blessings, these do not define the people who have them, any more than poverty defines those lacking them. What we do with what gifts we have, large or small, determines the person we are. It is from God that we know our true worth, and I think God finds us all very worthy, very lovable. As St. Francis of Assisi put it: "What do the world's scales know of your precious value?" This realization was a long time in coming to me, but I trust in its deep truth. I pray that I find ways to use my gifts to make a difference in the world.

When we return from Hobie Sound, I take Charlie for a walk through the campground looking for Monika's camp. I return without finding it, however. Later I realize there are two camping areas, but by then I have missed her and the chance to reconnect beyond our brief visit at the ranger station.

☘ ☘ ☘

The Florida Keys are amazingly beautiful and very popular this time of year. I would like to stay longer but should have reserved a State Park site months ago. We will stay in a private, much more expensive RV park so I'm only comfortable paying for two nights

Truly breathtaking aquamarine waters surround us as we drive down Highway 1, the Overseas Highway. When the sun slips behind a cloud, it changes the water to a rich turquoise with golden coral undertones. In the evening the water becomes deep jade green.

The Keys are not what I pictured: a series of 1,700 islands interconnected by long bridges or causeways. I had visions of driving over huge expanses of water but there are only a couple long bridges between Key Largo and Key West, the longest being seven miles. Many of the mangrove islands and hummocks are so close together that much of the time we drive over dry land. The Keys were first connected by a railroad built by Henry Flagler, who made his money in oil and then spent much of it in Florida developing hotels, churches, and resorts. His rail line was later converted to a highway

It isn't always clear where one key starts and another ends. In places channels separate them, but sometimes they seem to change name mid-island. Keith and I come up with some names in case any remain unnamed: Monk Key, Don Key, Malar Key, Hokey Po Key. It's possible there are unnamed keys since the mangroves create the islands and more could pop up from time to time.

We stop at a little roadside parkway to admire the water and let Charlie have an introduction to the Keys. A grizzled older man in a beat-up pickup is looking out at the water, watching the birds. He points to a bird he is watching and explains that frigate birds, about the size of crows with long scissor-tails, follow large fish and eat whatever is left when the fish devour prey. He says it is the season lemon sharks come into the shallows to spawn and believes the bird he points out is following a shark, looking for leftovers. The old man and the sea.

This is Hemingway country. He first moved here in 1928, when the only way to get here was by Henry Flagler's railroad or boat. While living here, he worked on *A Farewell to Arms, Death in the Afternoon, The Green Hills of Africa,* and a short story, *The Short Happy Life of Francis Macomber*. He wrote the only novel set in the United States, *To Have and Have Not*—thought to be based on people he knew in Key West—after he left. His home in Key West is a major tourist attraction.

Other notables who lived here include the artist Winslow Homer, who spent winters painting tropical watercolors. Harry Truman had a Little White House in Key West and a major road is named after him. Tennessee Williams moved here as a young man.

It is also Jimmy Buffet country—much of his music speaks to this area—the Keys and the Caribbean. He moved here in 1972 when he was in his mid-20s, just before recording his first successful album, *A White Sport Coat and a Pink Crustacean*.

As St. Augustine is the oldest, Key West is the farthest south you can drive and still be in the U.S. It is also the farthest place in the country you can drive from Portland: 3,400 miles by the shortest route, 3,900 by our route. The Bahamas are just east of here, Cuba just south.

The Keys are warm and tropical with temperatures this last week of March hitting the low 80s, cooling off to 70 at night.

We are staying on Grassy Key, about halfway down the keys, a bit of a drive to Key West, but we manage to visit twice during our short stay. We stop at a funky little place on Vaca Key called Herbie's to try conch fritters for lunch. The conch seems to be ground or chopped—the small pieces are still very chewy, similar to clam necks—mixed in batter and deep fried. These are another local delicacy I probably wouldn't eat regularly.

At Jim and Kathleen's recommendation, we stop at the Parrotdise Bar and Grill on Little Torch Key for some delicious jerked chicken wings, which we enjoy while gazing out at the turquoise water.

Judging from numerous large, expensive homes, there is plenty of wealth in the Keys, but there are and always have been less savory residents. During Hemingway's time, and when Jimmy Buffett first arrived, the Keys were a rough, hard-drinking area with minimal tourism but plenty of drug-running and smuggling activity.

I would love to spend a week or more here, time for kayaking, snorkeling—southern Florida is the only place in the Continental U.S. with coral reefs—or sailing. I hope to come back.

🌲 🌺 🌲

Leaving Key Largo, we drive through nurseries and cornfields, past produce stands already selling fresh fruits and vegetables, to the Tamiami Trail highway, which travels through the Everglades.

On the Tamiami highway, we follow a waterway and just past Big Cypress Visitor Center I spot my first two alligators. After that I see gators regularly, in the water or along the banks. Sighting them was exciting at first but soon becomes almost routine. The alligators I am seeing are big charcoal gray creatures.

"Wow, did you see those alligators?" I ask Keith when we pull over for a Charlie break.

"No, where? I haven't seen anything." The challenge in his voice tells me he doesn't quite believe me. He's been following in the Saturn as usual, and my higher vantage point gives me better views.

"I've seen some lying on the banks of the stream along the road," I say, feeling like I should apologize that he hasn't seen them, but reminding myself he chose to drive the Saturn.

After settling into our site at Collier-Seminole State Park near Naples—threading between trees that practically touch us on both sides—I suggest we hop back into the Saturn and backtrack to the Fakahatchee Strand State Park Boardwalk.

He starts to load Charlie in the car, and I shake my head.

"I think we'll leave Charlie in the Mo when we're exploring around here. Jim said the alligators are very dumb with a small prehistoric brain. But they move surprisingly quickly and are formidable killers."

At the Strand we walk across a bridge to the boardwalk, and I point out an alligator in the water. The boardwalk goes out into the cypress swamps, with signs explaining some of the flora and fauna. This area is home to Florida panthers, manatees and black bears, in addition to the alligators and millions of mosquitoes.

We walk a short distance, but the mosquitoes are vicious so we beat a hasty retreat. Even hurrying we spot another gator soaking in one of the algae-covered streams. I show it to a family walking ahead of us who had missed it. We also tell several people about the gator near the entry. We will come back later, armed with heavy-duty mosquito repellent.

Sunday we drive down to Everglades City and take a boat tour of the Ten Thousand Islands, part of Everglades National Park. We hope to see West Indian Manatees, endangered sea mammals that frequent these waters, but we are disappointed. We also don't see any of the rare American crocodiles that live in the salt-water marshes, though we really weren't expecting to be that fortunate. We enjoy seeing a variety of birds and a number of bottle-nosed dolphins. Our skipper encourages a pair of dolphins to chase our wake, and we get a delightful close encounter with these frolicsome, joyful creatures.

After the tour, we stop for dinner. Keith gets to satisfy his curiosity about alligator tail. It is small popcorn-type pieces deep-fried and is surprisingly good. We also sample hush puppies and fried sweet potatoes, which were mashed sweet potatoes formed into patties and then deep-fried; quite yummy. We finish it off with a shared piece of Key Lime pie. This is great southern comfort food.

On the way back we stop at the Fakahatchee Boardwalk and, under cover of mosquito repellent, venture to the end of the boardwalk, which offers views of the lush vegetation and a pond with baby alligators. It seems tropical with heavy undergrowth among the cypress and palms. The taller trees have bromeliads and air plants growing out of them. Birds with exotic songs and woodpeckers drilling into the trees fill the air with sound, and huge butterflies float by. It seems like another world, and I half-expect to see parrots or macaws or other brightly colored birds in the treetops, but the birds I see are plain brown and gray. It has been a beautiful day out in the Gulf and then in the swamps. Charlie is delighted when we come home to wake him from his nap on the dashboard and take him for a short walk.

This morning I woke up nearly as exhausted as when I went to bed last night. Maybe knowing we are moving again today kept me awake last night, struggling with anxiety. It felt suffocating, like I was buried deeply in Florida and fighting to get out.

After unhooking, checking maps and figuring out the route to our next destination, just outside of Orlando, we take off, again driving separately. Suzi Sunshine tries to cheer me up.

"It's okay, Maureen. It will be fine. You will be home soon, but you need to finish this trip. You need to see those places you've thought about: Savannah, Georgia, the Carolinas. John wanted you to see Virginia and Kentucky; do it for him if not for yourself. This may be the last time you'll have the chance. Last fall you turned tail and ran back home early. If you hadn't done that, you'd be finished with all of this and on your way home by now. You can do it, hang in there!"

"This traveling feels like such a burden sometimes," I groan, "more like torture than adventure."

"Well, remember," she's still trying to buoy me up, *"it's all about attitude. It's how we think about the things we're going through—how we view the future and the past more than what's actually happening in the present—that affects how we feel about things. So just focus on what's happening right this very moment and put on a happy face. Smile, smile, smile and send all that positive energy out into the Universe, and it will come back to you."* Suzi's a little into New Age feel-good energy things, but sometimes she makes sense.

"Yeah, I know I'm not being present to the present," I respond. "Lately I find myself dwelling on what to do when I return home. Will I need to find a job? Will I find a home I can afford to buy? Can I sell the Mo? And what about Keith?

"I'm pretty sure this won't work," I continue the dialogue with myself. "We fight over the silliest things. I'm so tired of explaining myself, of feeling like the person I am irritates him somehow. I think we've had more ridiculous fights in the few months we've been together than John and I had in 33 years of marriage. And Lance and I never fought, not even when he left me."

"Oh Lord, not Lance again," the Mother chimes in. *"You never spent more than a few hours with him; how do you know you wouldn't fight like cats and dogs if he were on this trip with you?"*

"I don't, and it's a pointless question since he's taken. I know that. It's just that we seemed much more compatible than Keith and I."

"Apparently he didn't agree," she says.

"Whatever. All I'm saying is, I don't see a future with a man who gets upset over what I consider silly things that are about who I am more than what I do."

"*Oh, you mean like the turtle incident?*"

"Yeah, that's one prime example. I see a turtle in the swamp and point it out to him. He gets all snarly with me. Didn't help when I explained to him that observing and pointing out wildlife was part of my family and my growing-up experiences."

"*Those were good times,*" Suzi reminisces. "*Dad taking the family for a drive in the country, seeing who would be the first to find a pheasant in the fields, or looking for deer farther up in the mountains.*"

"Yeah. Dad showing us wildlife and sometimes letting us point it out to him and feeling proud of us when we saw something first. It was sharing, making sure others saw the beauty in nature we found around us. For me it's a way of showing love, and it's part of me. It's second nature for me, when I see something I think is beautiful or awe-inspiring or even just interesting, to point it out to the people I am with. It doesn't mean I don't think they can't see it on their own; it means I want to invite them to share in the joy and beauty I find in it.

"I'll try to keep things smooth for the rest of our travels, but I don't see this going anywhere once we get back to our own spaces."

But Suzi's got a point. I don't need to—in fact I can't—make any of these decisions right now. Who knows how things will change, or how life will look, in another month or two or three. I need to work harder at living today, in the present moment, and not worry about next week or next month; it is only the present moment that exists. I should know this as well as anyone; life can be completely changed, for good or not so good, in one breath. It is in the present moment that we encounter God, in just being and waiting.

Though we stayed a week near St. Augustine, our previous stays have been anywhere from one night to four nights. That's a lot of hooking and unhooking and driving in the past five weeks.

Because I am writing posts for my own blog and *The Oregonian Travel* blog regularly, as well as articles for *The Oregonian* every three weeks, we have been total tourists. I've taken very little time to just sit, to read, to reflect. This was not my original intent. Undoubtedly some of my discomfort is the sense that I am letting myself down.

It's a balancing act: spending time experiencing the travel but finding time to process what I see, do and learn and consider how it affects me. Traveling with a partner requires a different kind of balancing: how do I do what I want to do, need to do, and still allow Keith to experience what he wants, have the down time he needs? Charlie doesn't care, as long as he gets to be with us. Dogs can teach us so much about appreciating the gifts of NOW.

Chapter 20
Flights of Fantasy

*You cannot wander anywhere that will not
aid you. Anything you can touch—God
brought it into the classroom of your mind.*
~ St. Francis of Assisi

"This is unbelievable!" I am looking out the window across a wide, grassy field after parking at the campground outside of Orlando. "It's Russ and Carol, my friends from Maine. That's their trailer, right across the field from us. Russ was just outside puttering around."

There are around 850 sites on several loops branching off the main road. I knew Russ and Carol would be here, but I hadn't yet checked to see which site they are in. They are parked only 100 yards from us.

"I'll be right back." I hook up Charlie's leash, and we wander across the field. Russ answers my knock and seems as surprised and delighted as I am when I greet him with a "Howdy there, neighbor!"

"Carol's down at the pool. Have you been there yet?" When I shake my head, he suggests we go meet her.

"Let me go see if Keith wants to come."

Keith declines so I return, and Russ, Charlie and I walk over to the pool to surprise Carol. He explains the layout of the campground points out that WiFi is available in the lodge next to the pool. We walk back to their trailer with Carol and make plans to get together later so they can meet Keith and suggest things to see and do here.

I've been to Disneyland twice but never Disney World, though Keith has been a couple of times. We talk about spending a day there.

"It's so expensive and I'm not sure I want to spend that much if I don't have kids to take. It's a make-believe place, and I am more interested in the real world," I say.

"I agree; it's too much money. I've been, but I thought you might enjoy it. Maybe when I meet Vivian later this week she can get us cheaper tickets." Keith is planning to visit a friend who works there.

Russ and Carol are knowledgeable guides; this is one of their destinations when they drive down every winter. They take me to Celebration, the master-planned community developed by the Walt Disney Company, for lunch and a tour. Again, Keith has elected not to join me as I spend time with my friends. After lunch we visit Downtown Disney, filled with shops and restaurants. From here you can catch a bus or a boat and travel around the Magic Kingdom.

🌲🌼🌲

Russ has offered to take Charlie for a walk while Keith and I visit the Cape Kennedy Space Center, a 90-minute drive back to the coast. It is fascinating, even for someone who has never been all that intrigued by space travel. The $40 tickets include a two-hour bus tour and program recounting 50 years of U.S. space exploration and a visit to the Apollo/Saturn V Center with the computer and communications equipment used in the Apollo missions command center.

We also tour the International Space Station Center, which provides information on the ongoing project.

The Kennedy Space Center is surrounded by the Merritt Island National Wildlife Refuge. We explore a little bit here—mostly because we take a wrong turn. During the Space Center tour, we saw a flock of roseated spoonbills—large long-legged birds with deep rose coloring on their wings—as well as many other birds. There is reportedly a healthy West Indian manatee population because the waters are closed to boats, which can kill or maim manatees. Still, we don't see any.

🌲🌼🌲

Charlie has his own close encounters with wildlife. A very large turtle lives in a hole about 100 feet from our door. A couple of times Charlie has darted out the door before I could grab him and run to investigate the hole to see if Mr. Turtle is home and wants to play. I suspect Mr. Turtle might be a snapper and could injure Charlie if he puts his head too deeply into the hole.

While Keith spends a day visiting Vivian in Kissimmee, I clean house, including hiring a company to wash the outside. It looks much better without thousands of miles worth of dirt covering it.

Our last two days in Clermont are filled with rain, thunder and lightning, which vindicates our decision not to visit Disney World. It's a warm, muggy rain rather than cool and refreshing, which we would have welcomed.

Florida is much bigger and more diverse than I imagined, with three National Parks—Everglades, Dry Tortugas, and Biscayne—and several national preserves, wildlife refuges, national seashores and marine sanctuaries. On the panhandle side, Florida stretches 350 miles from the border with Alabama to the Atlantic Ocean. More than 400 miles of coastline run from the northern border with Georgia to Key West. I have enjoyed nearly every inch we've explored, but after three weeks, it is time to say goodbye and begin our northward trek.

🌲🌿🌲

We drive through orange and grapefruit groves, past produce stands selling fresh strawberries, grapefruit, and Valencia oranges; the navels have already been harvested. We stop to sample the strawberries and they are tender, sweet and juicy.

Driving into Georgia brings relief with cooler temperatures. It's cloudy but doesn't seem as humid. I am wearing my jeans instead of the shorts and sleeveless shirts I've worn the past three weeks. Charlie is much happier with this cooler weather. I think the heat and humidity were hard on him.

Fort McCallister State Park in Richmond Hill, Georgia, is a little south of Savannah. Russ and Carol recommended we stay here while visiting this gracious southern city. The park is the remains of an old Civil War-era earthwork fort on the banks of the Great Ogeechee River, mostly tidal flats and marshes. This part of Georgia and the eastern part of South Carolina are known as "the Low Country." I presume that is because as we head west and north the altitude increases, and eventually we will be in the Appalachians and the Great Smoky Mountains.

A neighbor parked across from us visits with me as I tend our campfire while Keith takes a shower. He says he and his wife are from Minnesota. They became full-timers last December.

"The cost of diesel doesn't bother us too much," he explains. "We usually only travel about 100 miles at a time and stay for a week or so at each place."

Keith returns from the bathhouse, towel draped over his shoulders, and joins the conversation.

"There's a lot more to this RV lifestyle than I realized," he tells me after we've doused the fire and are settling in for the night. "I used to drive past these big motor homes on the highway and just thought they were wasting valuable resources, spending money, taking up too much room on the road. But now I understand these people may be driving their only homes down the road. It's just a whole different way of life, and most people have no idea what all is involved."

Keith has made similar comments a couple times during our travels, and he is right. Unless you've taken the time to explore the RV life a little, there is so much that lies below the surface. I've met people who live in their RVs and travel from workplace to workplace, and many who have no other home.

Clubs hold huge gatherings—jamborees—where people from all over gather to share information, reunite with old friends, learn more and just have fun. Programs and associations provide health coverage and other insurance, support, education and information. A variety of membership programs provide camping discounts. Aside from these programs, there is a wide range of places to stay from a few days in federal campgrounds with no amenities to all winter or summer in luxurious resorts in spaces people rent or own outright.

It's a lifestyle that gives people the freedom to live anywhere they want in some very beautiful places, even if only for a couple weeks at a time. It allows them to make friends all over the country. They visit friends and family and still have the comfort and convenience of their own private home and belongings. I like having my things with me, knowing what my bed is like and who slept in it last, being familiar with my kitchen, my equipment, having the food and supplies I need. It's comforting to Charlie, too, I think.

🌲🌺🌲

In the morning, we spend a couple of hours walking around Savannah, a glorious old dowager filled with restored antebellum homes, gardens, statues and fountains. Spanish moss drapes from the live oaks like shawls, and the dogwood and azaleas are blooming. With the sun shining and temperatures around 75°, it's hard to imagine a lovelier place to while away a few hours.

The Savannah Riverfront area is lined with old cotton warehouses that have been repurposed into shops. A brick walkway runs next to the river. Brick was a popular building element in Savannah: it was used in houses, walls, warehouses, even streets.

We sample pralines and other pecan-filled treats, and I buy a small can of Georgia peanuts, which are crunchy and sweet—far superior, in my opinion, to boiled peanuts.

Again we opt for a tour to learn more about this gracious Southern city. Savannah was originally developed by James Oglethorpe in 1733 in grids around a series of squares with 21 of the original 24 squares still remaining and well preserved. Many of the original settlers were brought to relieve the debtors' prisons in England and to establish a colony as a buffer between Spanish Florida and the rich Carolinas. Georgia was the last of the 13 original colonies.

Irish shops and pubs scattered throughout the city attest to the large influx of immigrants from the Emerald Isle. According to our tour guide, Savannah has the second-largest St. Patrick's Day celebration in the country, behind New York. The Irish workers were brought in (probably from those debtors prisons) to help with the cotton shipping and were given the most dangerous jobs loading the ships. Planters weren't willing to risk valuable slaves, and the Irish were considered easily expendable. This makes my Irish blood boil! They were disliked because they were Catholics, who were originally excluded from Savannah, along with lawyers.

Eli Whitney invented the cotton gin while working as a tutor in Savannah. Before that invention, rice was the major cash crop. When Whitney solved the problem of removing the seeds from cotton, it became a viable crop, and those who grew and traded cotton became wealthy and built beautiful homes, many of which remain.

On our last night at the campground, we enjoy a rendezvous with Russ and Carol who are staying here on their way back to Maine.

🌲🌵🌲

Leaving Georgia, we travel through South Carolina without stopping at Charleston. We land at a small RV park near Wilson, North Carolina, an hour east of Raleigh-Durham.

There isn't much in Wilson so during our free day here we explore the area east of us: Pamlico and Albemarle sounds and the southern Outer Banks. We head for Swan Quarter planning to take the ferry to Ocracoke. Some hundred miles later we arrive at the ferry and discover why there was no traffic coming or going on this route. During winter the ferry only runs at 9:30 a.m. and 4 p.m. daily. It is mid-day; we have missed the first and can't wait for the last ferry.

We drive northeast to Roanoke Island, then Bodie Island. The Outer Banks are a series of barrier islands that stretch south about 130 miles from the border with Virginia. There appears to be abundant beaches and sand dunes and plenty of huge houses for rent. Unlike the Florida Keys, not much is open in early April.

The names here are intriguing. Kill Devil Hills is named after the rum that washed ashore from the many shipwrecks (more than 2,000) in this area. The locals claimed this nasty rum "would kill the devil."

Nags Head was named after "the practice of tying a lantern to a horse and walking the beach, thus luring ships onto shore for plundering," according to the Outer Banks Official Travel Guide.

I'm curious about the source of the name for the University of North Carolina athletics program. I've asked several people and gotten several different answers. The term "Tar Heels" has some obscure beginnings but alludes to the tar, pitch and turpentine that were early products of North Carolina. Folklore claims that during the Civil War

General Lee praised the North Carolina soldiers for sticking to battle like they had tar on their heels. An alternative version claims Lee needed to put tar on the heels of other regiments who weren't as steadfast in their duties as the North Carolina soldiers.

The islands have a history of pirates, probably contributing to the nickname "Graveyard of the Atlantic." Edward Teach—Blackbeard the pirate—was beheaded in the waters off Ocracoke Island in 1718.

We stop at a beach south of Nags Head, but the wind is blowing so hard it feels like a sand blaster striking our bare legs and faces. We drive down to the Cape Hatteras Lighthouse, another 50 miles. It is the "tallest brick beacon" in the world, at 208 feet. We head back through the Alligator River National Wildlife Refuge.

The countryside is beautiful, mostly flat farmland with dogwoods, azaleas, and what looks like wild wisteria blooming abundantly. Along the freeways California poppies and other colorful wildflowers bloom.

Nearly 400 miles and nine exhausting hours later we return to the RV park, and I forage through my freezer, refrigerator and cupboards searching for something to fix for dinner. We tried to find some place to eat in Wilson but the "not much here" extends to any kind of restaurant or even a fast food place. Even Charlie—who loves going for rides—is happy to be back home. He's a patient dog, but sometimes I try his patience too much.

✿ ✿ ✿

A week ago we were touring Kennedy Space Center and reliving the accomplishments propelling mankind into space. Today we time-traveled backwards to Kitty Hawk to the first successful powered flight. Not quite 105 years ago, on December 17, 1903, Orville and Wilbur Wright successfully flew a small motor-powered airplane.

They spent their own money and time—several years— observing birds, researching previous attempts at flight and building kites and gliders to find better ways to control the machine. They built a wind tunnel and tested different techniques for wings and propellers. Finally, after numerous tests and experiments, Orville piloted the machine in its first flight of 12 seconds and 120 feet. They flew the machine three more times that day, with the final flight lasting 59 seconds and covering 852 feet.

"It is not really necessary to look too far into the future; we see enough already to be certain it will be magnificent. Only let us hurry and open the roads," Wilbur Wright said. One wonders if he had any idea where their first flight at Kill Devil Hills would eventually lead: to the moon, Mars and beyond. Sadly, he barely lived long enough to see his work come to fruition. Nine years after that first flight, he contracted typhoid fever and died at the age of 45. Orville lived to see many of the aeronautic advancements built on the brothers' work.

As I think about this I realize many of us will never see the fruits of our efforts. So often the results of things we do—good or bad—aren't readily apparent. We just have to keep doing what we feel called to do, have faith that our positive energy is being guided by Someone wiser, and trust that good will come, whether we ever know about it or not.

Before leaving the Outer Banks, we take a side trip to Norfolk and Virginia Beach, getting close enough to see Chesapeake Bay and say our final goodbyes to the Atlantic Ocean as we prepare to head inland tomorrow.

After his cross-country drive, John told me he wanted to take me to Virginia and Kentucky some day, which he found to be very beautiful. He thought I would like them too. This detour to see some of Virginia is done in his memory, and what I see is indeed beautiful. Ultimately, he did bring me here. I wonder if he knows that.

We will spend a few days in western North Carolina and then Kentucky will be next. I think John would be pleased.

Chapter 21
Following Mountains Home

What we call the beginning is often the end
And to make an end is to make a beginning.
The end is where we start from . . .
We shall not cease from exploration.
And the end of all our exploring
Will be to arrive where we started
And know the place for the first time.
~ T. S. Eliot

Driving across North Carolina to our next destination near Greensboro gives me time to stew over three unflattering letters *The Oregonian* received after my recent article on Louisiana. The writers found some of my observations uncomplimentary.

In spite of supportive and positive comments from my editor, I was unable to sleep most of last night, a reminder I'm still too thin-skinned and care too much what people think about me, even strangers.

I tell myself it doesn't matter what others think of me or expect me to do. What matters is being true to myself, finding my own meaning and authentic voice. People receive communication—oral or written—from their own perspective, and these folks just wanted to read something different from what I wrote. My job is to express what I experience and learn from this travel, not be a mouthpiece for others.

As I follow state routes through small towns and picturesque rural lands, the pastoral scenes of North Carolina calm me down. It is charming and a bit humble but beautiful. The dogwoods are showing off beautiful white blossoms. We have seen delicate-looking trees or large shrubs with purple-pink blooms that are unfamiliar; locals tell me it is redbud, which grows wild here.

The three letters that upset me are the only negative responses I've received to my traveling and writing; I've gotten plenty of positive feedback over these months. This realization brings better perspective, and I question my tendency to focus on negatives.

In my personal blog, I responded to the letters and several people who follow my blog wrote encouraging comments. One writer advised me not to worry about "those that get uppity about what they read and disagree with. Just keep putting finger to keyboard and let the masses do what they will. I, for one, will keep reading and using some of what you write as I strike out again, on the roads that make up this beautiful country."

Another noted: "I have been following along since January and can't wait to read each new blog. Also, I follow along in *The Oregonian*. You are living the life that I envy. Somehow, I wish I had the courage to leave the comfort of my home and travel the back roads and see this beautiful country. Keep doing what you are doing and don't let anything get you down."

It's good to know I am touching some people in positive ways; that makes it all worthwhile.

🌲🌸🌲

"Mountains!" Charlie perks up his ears when he hears the excitement in my voice. It seems so long since I've seen mountains, and I am delighted with the view of the Blue Ridge Mountains. Surrounded by them in Oregon, I undoubtedly take them for granted. I have been deprived of high vistas since we drove through New Mexico several weeks ago. I love that they draw my eyes up, raising my spirits, and I take a moment to say a quiet thank you to their Creator.

Since reading Catherine Marshall's *Christy* as a teenager I have been curious about this Smoky Mountain area. The mountains here aren't as steep as the Rockies or the Cascades. They're not craggy or high, snow-capped peaks. But they are beautiful, row upon row of tall hills, rounded, smooth and covered in trees. We discover very little is level when we park the Mo at the RV park south of Sylva: even with all my leveling blocks we still list a bit.

This is a pleasant area, with a fairly temperate climate, although it supposedly gets more rain than either Portland or Seattle. It seems reasonably affordable. Locals tell us people who live in Florida during the winter often come here for cooler summers.

"We call 'em half-backs," says a woman from Gainesville who is currently staying at the RV park. "They moved from the cold north down to Florida for the warmth. But then they can't take the heat and humidity in the summer so they move half-way back north."

The residents of this RV park are friendly; I think most are here fairly long-term, and they are helpful in suggesting where to go and what to see. The mostly deciduous forests are beginning to leaf out; next week is the Greening Up festival in Sylva. We can still see most of the form and curves of the terrain, the steep drives that get residents up to their homes perched high on these hills.

We take Charlie on walks along winding country roads up into the hills, following a lovely, chattering stream. There is obvious poverty here, with numerous mobile homes and trailers, tiny shacks and cabins in the draws, but also beautiful log homes with sweeping views.

🌲🌼🌲

Friday we drive to Asheville and spend most of the day touring the home to end all homes: the overwhelming Biltmore Estate. It is so huge and takes so long to see, we have no time to see anything else in Asheville.

I splurge on the audio tour and share what I am hearing with Keith, repeating and summarizing facts on the tape I think he might enjoy.

"Biltmore has 250-rooms and was the country estate of George Washington Vanderbilt, grandson of wealthy shipping and railroad tycoon Cornelius Vanderbilt. It took six years to build.

"When George was 33, the mansion was completed, and he held a grand opening on Christmas Eve, 1895. It remains the largest privately owned home in the U.S. with four stories, 65 fireplaces, an indoor swimming pool and bowling alley, among other luxuries.

"Man, I can't believe how big these rooms are; some seem as large as a modest house! This place is amazing and opulent and decadent! And kind of disgusting." I throw in some opinions along with the facts.

"About 8,000 acres are left of the original 125,000, with formal and informal gardens designed by Frederick Law Olmstead who also designed Central Park in New York and the Capitol Grounds in Washington, D.C."

About this time Keith walks away from me. I suspect he thinks I am lecturing him again, telling him things he wants to figure out on his own. Repeating information is a way of imprinting it more strongly in my own memory, but when it becomes evident he doesn't appreciate my sharing, I just listen for myself.

We arrived in time for the Festival of Flowers display and wander the gardens and greenhouses. I enjoy the acres of brilliant tulips and flowering trees and shrubs much more than I enjoyed the house and its furnishings.

Such extravagance is uncomfortable for me to view; I wonder if this was an attempt to create his own heaven on earth. I confess I don't see the need for 33 bedrooms or 43 bathrooms in one home. My family of eight had three bedrooms and shared one bathroom. While that was inadequate, Biltmore is just overwhelming. Of course it was meant to impress; perhaps George wanted to do something more than his father or grandfather. But I am being judgmental and coming from a viewpoint of scarcity rather than abundance. The construction of Biltmore created jobs and opportunities for this area and his support of the arts is commendable. Vanderbilt also supported a number of charities and literacy efforts, including one of the first public libraries and a teacher's college in New York.

🌲🌿🌲

We spend Saturday viewing the natural beauty of the Great Smoky Mountains National Park and Blue Ridge Parkway. The Parkway begins in the National Park and wends its way across mountains 469 miles north into Virginia. We drive about a dozen miles and exit through Maggie Valley since there is still snow on parts of the Parkway.

These mountains—part of the Appalachian chain that stretches down from Canada—got the name "Smoky" because of the abundance of mist and wisps of clouds that drift up out of the "hollers" and "cricks," undoubtedly a result of the humidity in the area. This morning we awoke to rain and clouds; mist and fog shrouded the mountaintops (tallest at about 6,000 feet). Then the sun popped out and added another dimension to the landscape.

The roads we follow are lined with wildflowers including trillium, redbud and dogwood. Numerous streams and rivulets cascade down the slopes to the river, a shallow, fast-moving, clear stream full of rapids and waterfalls. The ground is carpeted with brown leaves from last fall. The hills and valleys, water and flowers are, for me, an abundance of beauty more breathtaking than any of Biltmore's riches.

Tomorrow, April 20, our visit to North Carolina will end when we drive through Tennessee and into Kentucky.

🌲🌿🌲

"My attorney says I need to get back to Tacoma as soon as possible," Keith, sitting at the dinette in the Mo, tells me after a phone conversation Tuesday afternoon, our second day in Lexington. Keith has been dealing with a professional issue that surfaced while we were in Florida. "He thinks it would be better if I were there to handle this personally." He rests his forehead on his hands, clearly frustrated and apologetic.

"Well, how do you want to do that?" I ask, laying a hand on his shoulder. "We could put you on a plane if you need to be back quickly, and I can just drive back by myself. Or we can just wait a couple more days and drive back together. I've already paid for five nights here, and I doubt they'll give me a refund. I'd like to see the Museum of the Horse and spend some time with Tina while I'm here. I can do that tomorrow."

Tina is Kristin's friend who is currently earning her PhD in gerontology at the University of Kentucky here in Lexington. I also want a little more time to explore the Blue Grass State, one I've always wanted to visit, especially since I've loved horses all my life.

"So, is Friday soon enough?"

"How long would it take if we just head home from here?" he asks.

I get out my atlas and do some quick estimating. "I think we could make it home in a little over a week if we skip Tennessee, Arkansas and Oklahoma and head across country. Ten days at the longest. So say May 2 or 3, maybe earlier, depending on weather and how long we are willing to drive every day. Is that soon enough?"

"I guess it will have to be." He shrugs. "I'm sorry you'll miss some of the places you've never seen."

I've been looking forward to visiting Nashville and Memphis. I want to spend time in northern New Mexico. We just passed through the southern tip on our way east because I believed we'd be spending time there on our way back. I'd also been hoping to spend time in Utah and Colorado.

"I guess those places will have to wait for another time," I say, waving my hand dismissively. "Truthfully, I'm looking forward to going back home.

"When I was traveling alone last fall, it was clear when it was time for me to head home. It seems that's happening again. It'll be fine." I pat his shoulder.

🌲🌼🌲

The Kentucky Horse Park in Lexington, recommended by Jim and Kathleen, has been a pleasant surprise, another state park worth visiting. It is quiet and relaxed with large paved parking sites surrounded by acres of soft green grass neatly mowed. The polo field up the road is a large open area where dogs are allowed to be off-leash. There are almost as many dogs as horses here. Down the hill from the polo field is the steeplechase field with jumps set up.

The campground is next to the Kentucky Horse Park exhibit area, so Keith and I walk over to check it out. I am excited to learn that the Rolex Three-Day Event, a pre-qualifier for the U.S. Olympic equestrian team, starts Thursday; I hope to be able to see some of the events. Before John and I had children, we had horses, and I studied dressage for several years. I trained and showed my part-Arab mare in basic dressage, English, halter and driving classes. It was an expensive hobby, so when it was time to start our family, I sold the horses.

The International Museum of the Horse has fascinating displays and information on the history and evolution of the horse and its contributions to civilization, with a particular focus on horses in America's history.

"Wow, this is interesting! I didn't know Paul Revere was one of three riders who were trying to warn the Colonial militia of the approaching British soldiers. Says here he and another rider were apprehended by the British before they could complete their mission. It was the third rider who was ultimately successful in setting off the alarm, and he shall apparently be lost to history because…well, who knows?"

"Maybe because Longfellow didn't write about him," Keith suggests. "Maybe Paul Revere was easier to rhyme for poetry, or he just had a better PR person, someone who could spin his story better than that other guy."

I spend the next day with Tina. We drive out to Keeneland Racetrack, where we take photos of each other trying on $200 hats in the gift shop. We drive along the Bluegrass Parkway and follow the Bourbon Trail, though all the distilleries are closed. Since we don't find any distilleries open, we stop at a bar for an obligatory mint julep. We agree we're not likely to ever order another.

On Thursday Keith, Charlie and I wander over to the Rolex competition to watch competitors from Australia, Canada and Great Britain, as well as the U.S. Our camping fees don't include admission to the competitive events so we watch riders warm up, see the dressage competition from a distance and observe an interesting variety of people and horses.

🌲🌼🌲

Friday morning I'm glad to be leaving the Horse Park; it has become busy, crowded and noisy. In addition to all the horse rigs now parked in the campground, the parking lots at the event center are full, and fields around the campground are filling up with cars.

In an effort to make better time, we tow the Saturn, and Keith and I take turns driving. By about 5 p.m., 470 miles later, we arrive via southern Indiana and Illinois, in Columbia, Missouri, for the night. I am relieved to stop; the wind has hindered us most of the day.

The next leg is unclear, and I'm studying maps to determine the best route west. It's still cold and snowy in Wyoming, so I-80 may not be the best option. But a more southerly route brings the possibility of tornadoes. For now it seems wisest to keep our options open and watch weather forecasts.

Saturday opens with sunshine and warmth, but as we continue west across the middle of the country, the wind picks up and remains a huge obstacle. Late in the day a wild blustery wind sweeps across the Kansas plains, accompanying us the rest of the afternoon. It blows the awning over the door loose, causing it to flap open and closed, something I've never experienced before. We stop twice to try to lock it and finally tape it shut with duct tape. We may just leave it taped till we get to Portland.

We stay on I-70 and at the end of our second long day are in Oakley, Kansas, just east of the Colorado state line. It's winter here with freezing temperatures after we've spent weeks in the 70s, 80s, and even 90s.

Sunday morning the storm warnings continue, and ultimately I choose to drive north out of Kansas into North Platte, Nebraska, and connect with I-80. I pray we miss the worst of the weather.

Almost all of our 510 miles this third day are directly into the wind, especially challenging when we are climbing up the 8,640 feet high "hill" between Cheyenne and Laramie. I expected mountains but this is high plains and buttes. Scattered snow lies on the ground, though it looks old and the road is clear, so I relax.

Between the headwind and the climb, we get terrible mileage, and this leads to an unpleasant experience. We pull off at an exit advertising diesel, but when I turn into the station's driveway, a chain blocks the entry and there is no room to turn around. Inch by inch, backing a little—very tricky with the Saturn attached—pulling forward a little, with Keith outside watching my corners and by the grace of God, I finally manage to get turned around. I slip between a couple of sign posts and under a telephone guy wire I'm not confident we'll clear to get back to the road. It has taken 15 minutes and plenty of patience. It would have been easier and quicker to unhook the Saturn, which would have greatly improved my maneuverability. Why am I so stubborn sometimes, I ask myself.

Diesel isn't as expensive in Wyoming as in other places; by that I mean it's less than $4.20 a gallon, but still $2 a gallon more than when we started in February. I am easily spending $250 a day on fuel. I suspect the cost will continue rising, so maybe it's better to be traveling home now than in another month or two.

Monday morning we finish our trek across Wyoming and head into Utah where we connect with I-84. We press on into Idaho, barely taking time to admire the Wasatch Mountains. We are definitely on the last leg, and I am feeling euphoric. Or maybe just exhausted from our 500-mile days, nine to ten hours of solid driving. Just as it felt last

October, I am racing against the weather, trying to get through the areas where there is still a threat of snow while we can. It's been good to have Keith to help spell me on the driving, but even with stops every two or three hours, it has been a breakneck pace.

Tuesday morning we drive through the southern part of Idaho, and I enjoy the pastoral scenes with circle irrigation farms—already the sprinklers are running and the hay and grain are a rich green. We drive through Boise and then Caldwell, the town where I was born, though I was raised in Central Washington. I smile seeing occasional Oregon license plates.

And then we are in Oregon. What can I say about this state that I've lived in for 30 years? Driving across the border, I feel like the prodigal daughter returning home to find love. Not even the most expensive diesel we've seen the whole trip ($4.38 a gallon), vicious winds in the Columbia River Gorge, or rain that falls off and on from Baker City west dampen my enthusiasm at being home.

The normally brown hills are green with cheatgrass that will soon turn golden. The green is dotted with yellow sunflowers, purple lupine and smaller blue and lavender forget-me-nots. The Blue Mountains and the Cascades still have snow on the higher peaks. Then driving into the Gorge, with wisps of clouds and fog hanging on the peaks, the moss clinging to the rocks—Oh my gosh. I'm home! And it's beautiful. Even the rain is beautiful. It's MY rain. I feel like George Bailey after his "dream." Hello, you wonderful Multnomah Falls! I love you, Oregon rain. Crown Point, I've missed you.

At about 5:30 Tuesday we pull into the RV park I have stayed at when I am in Portland. To say I am relieved and happy would be huge understatements; ecstatic is more appropriate.

Like Dorothy in *The Wizard of Oz*, whom I thought of while driving through windy Kansas, I kept telling myself; "There's no place like home." And now I'm here.

Many challenges still face me. I have no home, other than this one, no furnishings. I don't know what I will do. I will be starting over from scratch. But I have learned that life can only happen one step at a time, just like heading home was one day, one state, one city, one mile at a time. Returning to Oregon is the first step of my next journey.

Epilogue
Two Years Later

The story that we bring back from our journeys is
the boon. It is the gift of grace that was passed to us
in the heart of our journey.
~ *Phil Cousineau*

e returned to Portland the evening of April 29, nearly three
months after leaving. By Memorial Weekend, Keith and I agreed
the drama in our relationship precluded our survival as a couple.
Though a number of things worked well, and we had shared some
wonderful adventures, it was clear that our future would best continue
as friends and not as lovers.

I recently reread my journals from the fall and winter we were
getting to know each other. In a flash of insight, I realized that in my
mind I had created Keith to be someone I wanted him to be. I didn't
take the time to get to know and love the real person Keith is. When
he failed to accommodate my expectations and be my perfect match, I
felt frustrated and disappointed. That wasn't fair to him or to me.
Perhaps—much as I longed for a partner—I simply was not ready for
one yet. Apparently I still had more interior work to do.

Shirley accepted a job in Southern Oregon, and I was delighted to
have her within a few hours' drive. In mid-June, I met her in Medford
to help her find a home. This motivated me to look for a house myself,
and I found a small 1964 ranch-style home on a large lot in the suburbs
of Portland. It had space for Charlie to chase balls and squirrels, room
for a garden and room to park the Mo while I waited to get it sold.

On June 25 my role in life changed again as my first biological
grandchild, Jesse John, was born. As I held this precious child in my
arms, I asked John to watch over the child named in his memory. He
would have been dancing for joy to see his first grandchild, and maybe
he was.

That same day my house closed, and two months after returning to
Oregon, I moved out of the Mo into the first house I'd ever bought by

myself and began making it my own. I painted inside and out, refinished and replaced flooring, reinsulated the home and built raised beds for my garden, doing as much as possible by myself or with help from family.

Charlie did get to see Nick again, and was delighted to take a couple more walks with his buddy; but it was to say goodbye. Nick was dying. Shortly after we returned, Tom had Nick put to sleep. At 14 he had lived a long and full life and brought Tom much joy and love.

🌲 🌼 🌲

If I were measuring the success of my year of pilgrimage in financial terms, it would be a total disaster. Between the poor economy and the cost of diesel, the RV market was glutted with new and used rigs, several manufacturers went bankrupt, and RV values plummeted. More than a year after returning to Portland, I finally sold the Mo at a 33 percent loss. The $13,000 I spent for campground memberships was a total loss, and the Saturn suffered a lingering but terminal engine failure within a few months of returning, another complete loss.

I have tried to be philosophical about the losses and accept that most life lessons come with a cost. This year was my version of the treasure buried in the field, the pearl of great price, parables recorded in Matthew's Gospel, 13:44-45. The treasure I sought and sacrificed so much for was me, seeking the seed planted in my heart. Knowing our hearts, loving and becoming the person God created us to be, is indeed a treasure beyond price.

When I started in May of 2007, I sought a desert journey, time and solitude to travel more deeply inside myself to discover who I am and what I want to do with the rest of my life. Transformation happens slowly, incrementally, often indiscernibly, and is difficult to measure. Sometimes others see the changes before we do, and my friends have told me they see many changes in me.

Accomplishing goals we set for ourselves instills confidence, one change I can see in myself. I am thankful I had the opportunity—both the time and the financial resources—to make this journey. Knowing I set out on an ambitious, difficult challenge and saw it through empowers me and gives me the courage to tackle future difficult tasks.

More and more I like the person I discovered during my journey. The Mother, along with all her helpers, is still there, and sometimes I listen, but now I often pat her on the head, as Karl sometimes does to me, and say with love, acceptance and a little patronizing air, "Thanks, Mom. We're okay and all shall be well."

On both my extended trips, getting close to home and seeing Oregon license plates again felt like a hug from an old friend. I know this is where I want to live, at least for now. There are many wonderful places in our country, in our world, but Oregon feels like home to me, my right place for right now.

I brought few souvenirs home from my journeys. My best keepsakes are a new awareness, different ways of looking at the world. I have a new respect for people throughout the country. I now see life with more compassion, understanding and tolerance. I have learned more about beauty and being thankful for all of creation.

I have seen incredible places and better understand the geography of my country. I have met and talked with people from all regions, sampled wonderful local dishes, and some not so wonderful. I experienced local cultures and learned what makes different parts of this country so distinct. That has helped me better understand others' beliefs and what is important to them.

It seems to me that when we keep our world small and controlled, we keep our God small. By going out into the world, seeing and appreciating all of God's creation, we have a better understanding of the generosity and limitlessness, the grandeur of our Creator.

My travel reaffirmed my opinion that we Americans have so much in common if only we would take the time to look beyond the labels and listen to each other. The divisive politics that seem to be crippling our elected officials continues to worsen. This politics of hatred and name-calling sickens me. We are a wonderful and blessed nation, but our problems will never be solved unless we learn to listen and talk civilly and without rancor. We must find ways to understand each other better and work together. We must let go of labels and begin to love and respect each other even if we don't always agree.

I learned that reading maps can be very helpful when you need to get somewhere in a hurry, but going off the map can lead to unexpected adventures and beauty. I think this is a good lesson for life: skip the usual paths, the well-worn roads, and strike out on the one that speaks to your heart, no matter what others expect of you.

I recognize I am not perfect and never will be; I'm still a work in progress. I make mistakes but am learning to be kinder and more forgiving to myself and others, and move on without overly obsessing. When we stop growing, stop learning, stop moving towards God, we begin to atrophy. That is the beginning of death.

I continue to pursue my self-knowledge and take time for reflection and prayer. Since returning I've studied the mystics and their deep relationship to God. I took classes based on Martha Beck's *Steering by Starlight*, and Julia Cameron's *Artists Way*. I studied the Enneagram, an ancient spiritual tool for understanding personality types and using self-observation to identify barriers to contemplation.

I joined a dream group, studying and interpreting our dreams. Dreams can be messages about our lives our deeper self, our subconscious, is trying to get us to pay attention to.

I studied secular work on thought transformation by Byron Katie and others. I connected with an intuitive massage therapist to help me get in better touch with my body, learning to understand its cues. Again, these are tools to pay better attention to the whisperings God sends through subtle means.

Understanding better the consequences of how we spend our thoughts and energy, I accept that I can choose to use positive thinking for good and make a difference in the world just by the way I react to life. In the past, I often used my energy and thoughts in negative ways, to tear down myself and others, interpret others' responses to me in hurtful ways, or focus on doubts, fears and insecurities. By letting go of negative views of the world, I am more open to creativity and love

Have I touched any lives, made a difference for anyone? I don't know, but I know many people touched my life during my journey—even more have touched Charlie. Literally. Has he made a difference, besides to me, which goes without saying? It's hard to tell when a friendly smile or touch can make a difference to someone. I suppose that's something I never will know and maybe don't need to know. I gratefully accept the possibility that Charlie and I might have given someone a smile or lightened a heart.

🌲🌿🌲

One of the important lessons I have learned over these past three years is that I don't need a man to rescue me. I sometimes struggle with loneliness and occasionally long for a life partner to share the joys and sorrows, the straight, smooth highways and the detours of life. But I know I don't "need" a man. I have many friends who love me; I am blessed with a wonderful family. I am no longer controlled by the belief that the absence of a man in my life somehow diminishes me. I can take charge of my own life and be happy and fulfilled alone, whole and complete on my own, if that is what lies ahead on my path. More and more I am accepting that probability. I think as I become more open and pliable to whatever God has in store, my satisfaction with my life increases. I am beginning to live in God more, allowing God to fill those empty places in my heart.

While I recognize I need to be with people, I also need solitary time to pray, to just be with God, to listen and contemplate God's love.

As a result of this year of traveling, I am learning not to worry as much what other people think of me. Doing something outside of expectations, like selling everything, buying a motor home and driving it around the country, helped me break out of that need to fit in, helped me define myself on my own terms.

Ultimately I am the only person whose opinion of me truly matters. I can never control what others think, and I don't even need to know or worry about others' thoughts. That's not my business to attend to. I have to be secure in myself and let people think whatever they want. I can trust that the truth within me, placed there by a benevolent and wise God, will guide my steps. What freedom such letting go brings!

It didn't take long after my return to Portland to encounter Lance. I had mixed feelings, but over the ensuing months we had several opportunities to talk. The insurmountable goal of being friends we'd sought three years earlier is being realized. We both have changed and grown, and I think we feel more comfortable with each other and our changing relationship.

Though I would not have believed it possible, in some ways I feel a deeper connection and love for him than before, less passion and more compassion. We share a painful but tender history that will never go away. I love him as a person, not the imaginary dashing but unattainable hero who abandoned me three years ago. Our affection for each other feels more mature and peaceful. I'm not sure I could ask for a better outcome than his friendship.

When I allow myself to listen to my stories about how happy we could have been if things had turned out differently, I still feel moments of longing and regret. During these times, I am thankful my growth and self-exploration allow me to understand these are stories, not reality. Reality is that, though we were apparently not meant to be a team, we can still love each other. Knowing myself allows me to better live with that tension and cherish this friendship as a grace in my life.

My work with a new spiritual director steeped in Ignatian spirituality has helped me understand that, just as I had the strength to meet challenges during my year of traveling and self-exploration, I have the power to find peace and fulfillment as his friend and let go of unhealthy attachments.

This work is a little easier because a new relationship fills my life with joy, laughter and love: my grandson Jesse. He and Karl have become an ongoing presence in my life and brought unexpected companionship and purpose. As I hold Jesse, listen to his laughter, see his smiles, rock him to sleep, I feel incredibly close to John and the love we shared that brought our children and now Jesse into being. It is a reminder that those we love continue to live on in many ways. John's blood flows through Kristin, Karl and Jesse, and the legacy he dreamed of is achieved.

As I become more in touch with my true self through quiet contemplation and reflection, I learn to better love myself and find I have more patience with others. I have learned to see the world from softer eyes, and I can let go of unimportant things and better appreciate the humor and joy in life. It feels a little like being in love: Things looks a little different, colors are brighter, my sense of humor and enjoyment are keener. Maybe I fell in love with life itself. I set out to try to fall in love with God; falling in love with life is a way of falling in love with God.

I continue to pursue that deeper love, though sometimes it evades me, or perhaps I evade it. I continue to seek God's presence in my life and where and how God's love is calling me to serve, helping make a difference in others' lives. I've explored the possibility of volunteering with Jesuit Refugee Services or other similar programs helping people whose lives have been so terribly uprooted by wars or natural disasters, though work abroad will have to wait until Charlie is no longer in my life. Again, I am trying to stay open to inspiration.

I imagine God as the "Life Star" with a huge tractor beam, continually pulling us all towards Love. I have been blessed to feel that pull all my life. As I continue my journey, I know whatever work I do must somehow incorporate an effort to help others experience that all-embracing love.

Could it be that my sole purpose—all our souls' purpose—is merely to observe, contemplate and celebrate God's generous beauty, to accept God's love? Could my role in life, my destiny, be simply to reflect on and reflect the beauty of creation, the love of our Creator? I can do that as a writer, as a poet, as a photographer, and perhaps that is enough. To love and experience beauty and joy and share it with others—what better calling is there?

Reflecting on your epitaph, what might be carved on your gravestone when you die, is a valuable exercise. I think I'd like people to remember me this way: She was like the ocean, wide and deep, beautiful and mysterious, always changing but ever-constant, nurturing and full of life, touching many with gentle caresses but powerful and just a little dangerous. Or even more simply: She loved greatly and was loved.

This year, as every year since John died, I tried to ignore Valentine's Day, a very challenging day for me and for most people who don't have "a valentine." Driving to a meeting on February 13, I saw the street vendors selling bouquets of flowers and felt a tinge of sadness knowing I wouldn't get flowers again this year. Or chocolates, or anything the advertisers tell us we need to remind us we are loved.

Suddenly I realized I am loved. I have Someone who loves me unconditionally, who delights in me, who adores me. So I asked God to be my valentine, and God responded: "I thought you'd never ask!" The next day as I walked Charlie, I was touched by the beautiful spring flowers God put in my path.

Could I not have figured some of these things out for myself, without the expense and time, the sacrifice and challenges of this year of journeying? As the Sufi mystic, Rumi, writes:

> I will hunt for the Beloved with all my power
> And all my strength and passion until I know
> It is futile to look for Him.
> Yet how could I know His Presence near me
> Without traveling across the world?
> How could I grasp Its sublime Mystery
> Without risking a long journey?
> God has told us He is with us
> But has sealed the heart
> So it cannot understand this
> Except slowly and indirectly.
> When you have accomplished many journeys
> And fulfilled the Path's duties,
> The seal will then be withdrawn from your heart.
> Then you'll say to yourself, "If I'd known
> I was always so extremely near to God
> How would I have been able to look for Him?"
> Yet this knowledge depended on a journey;
> Sharpness of mind alone could never win it.

I have been searching for the Beloved all my life. Sometimes I go forward, sometimes I get stuck, unable to move, as I was in the parking lot in Omaha. Now I now I just have to wait. Occasionally friends are there to support and guide me through difficult places, but ultimately this is a journey I must allow God to accomplish in me. It requires my willingness to abandon myself in God, and this requires prayer.

In Chapter 6 of Matthew's Gospel, Jesus calls us to be like the birds of the air, the lilies of the field, and not to worry about our physical welfare: our food and drink, our clothing. Seek first and foremost the Kingdom of God and be concerned "with what He requires of you," and God will take care of the less important things. This is one of the most difficult and challenging things Jesus calls us to. Give up your concern with living well, looking well, being well fed, and focus on me and the Father.

As hard as it is to think about turning our physical needs over to God, how much more difficult is it to allow God to direct our spiritual affairs? The mystics tell us in their writings that the Dark Night of the Soul is a process of letting go of our need to control our spiritual lives. It is abandoning ourselves completely to God in prayer. Contemplation is not emptiness, it is not nothingness; it is God whispering to us of love. It is asking God and then allowing God to take away our distractions, our compulsions, our attachments, our beliefs, our securities, and leaving us a clean vessel to be filled with God's love.

This is the loss of "self" that happens through the Dark Night of the Soul/Spirit. Little by little we are able to give up things that we have held dearly that have seemed critical to our spiritual well being, our very identity. Perhaps these are our false gods, idols that keep us from knowing God, even if they have always seemed holy and good. These old attachments can be barriers that bind us to a limited understanding and knowledge of God.

If we focus on directing our own thoughts, mind and will, we don't leave room for God's part of the conversation. There is security in following a plan, a map. By saying the right things at the right times, we feel we're crossing the t's and dotting the i's of prayer, getting it right. Certainly formal prayers like *The Our Father* have a place in our tradition. But so does contemplation.

In *The Naked Now: Learning to See as the Mystics See,* Richard Rohr writes about Jesus' views on prayer found in several Gospel references. Jesus warned against "public" or "standing" prayer. His words and example taught that prayer should be private, quiet and personal. In fact, Rohr indicates that Luke's Gospel story of Jesus teaching *The Lord's Prayer* implies he only gave them a verbal prayer because they begged for one.

Consider the birds of the air, the lilies of the field, the tall trees, the mountains, even the golden retriever lying at my feet. They do not worry about how they pray. Their every breath, their very being is a prayer. They live in the freedom of being who or what God created them to be. I want to be able to let God lead the dance; God knows the steps far better than I ever will.

Through prayer, contemplation, awareness of the experiences and people God puts in my path, I can move closer to my own right path. Always I know a loving and benevolent God is there; I am learning to trust in that Presence, to have faith that wherever I am supposed to be going, I will be led.

I don't believe God is a present you open on Christmas morning and suddenly life is perfect and joy is always at your side. My faith life is more like opening small presents every day, each one unfolding some new and precious aspect of God. Sometimes the meaning of these gifts isn't immediately clear. I must hold them in my heart, dwell with them, live in the mystery, always trusting there is a purpose. It is always challenging; wrong turns and shortcuts are abundant and attractive and may seem easier. These misleading choices ultimately make me more lost and confused.

When we are lost, we are supposed to stay in one place and wait to be found. Waiting is hard! It requires great faith, patience and trust that we will be rescued, that the way will be revealed. God has promised never to forget us; I continue to ask God to give me the courage and patience to trust in that promise.

St. Ignatius of Loyola wrote a beautiful prayer, the Suscipe: "Take, Lord, and receive all my liberty, my memory, my understanding and my entire will, all I have and call my own. You have given all to me. To you, Lord, I return it. Everything is yours; do with it what you will. Give me only your love and your grace, that is enough for me."

I pray for the courage to seek only God's grace and love, knowing that if I can accept those gifts and abandon my desires for the things my ego wants, all will be well, and I will reach the destination I set out for. Then joy and peace will be my traveling companions.

So where will the roads of my life lead me next, I wonder. What graces still await as I move through my 60th year into mystery and joy? Life is an ongoing gift, and I look forward to continuing the journey.

178

ACKNOWLEDGEMENTS

My deep appreciation and love to family and friends who supported me, both during the devastating loss of John, and my year of journeying. Most especially I thank my children, Kristin Hovenkotter Greco and Karl Hovenkotter, for the graces they have brought me and for allowing me the privilege of being their mother. My thanks to all who helped me prepare for and accomplish the journey to try to find myself.

Special thanks to Marilyn Kirvin and Barb Scharff, true companions on this journey. They listened to my doubts, held me in my pain, faithfully read my blog, and provided support, helpful suggestions and positive encouragement during my travels and throughout the writing of this book. Other wonderful friends who have been there for me during much of this journey, often propping me up or giving me a shoulder to cry on, include Katie Hennessy, Colleen Wagner, Julie Dale, Shelli Romero and Kathleen Coleman. I treasure their friendship and that of so many other people.

I received helpful insight and perspective on the book from a number of people. In addition to Kristin, Karl, Marilyn, Barb and Julie, Marilyn Veomette, Suzanne Dillard Burke, Tony Staley, Janet Buck, Ross Eberman, Bobbi Fisher, Mary Farina and Shirley Gray read all or parts of the manuscript. Additional thanks to two friends who provided early editing assistance and feedback on the book: Margo Peifer and Russ Burbank; and to Sherold Barr and Gail Cunningham for their helpful advice and encouragement. Tora Koneko, a young graphic artist, did a beautiful job designing the cover using a photo I took while driving through Utah on the journey, and I thank her.

The spiritual aspects of this journey are largely the fruits of my membership in St. Ignatius Parish and result from the inspiration of members of the Oregon Province of the Society of Jesus, the Jesuits. I am especially grateful to Fr. Peter Byrne, SJ, whose spiritual depth and insight in the years following John's death provided me with a map to follow. Other critical spiritual guides have included Jack Kennedy, my current spiritual director, and Sr. Frances Madden, SNJM, my SEEL director.

I'm forever grateful to Kerry Tymchuk for taking a risk and providing me the amazing opportunity to work for Senator Gordon Smith. Kerry has always been generous with his time, enthusiastic, willing to listen and offer assistance, contacts and encouragement. He introduced me to Ross Eberman of Carpe Diem Books who provided helpful professional advice, invaluable guidance and contacts. Ross connected me to my final editor, Jill Kelly, to whom I extend great appreciation for her thoroughness, insightfulness and patience.

BIBLIOGRAPHY/REFERENCES

Traveling Souls: Contemporary Pilgrimage Stories, Whereabouts Press, 1999

The Art of Pilgrimage: The Seeker's Guide to Making Travel Sacred, Phil Cousineau, Conari Press, 1998.

Travels with Charley in Search of America, John Steinbeck, Viking Press, 1962

Steering by Starlight: Find Your Right Life No Matter What, Martha Beck, Rodale, Inc, 2008

When the Heart Waits: Spiritual Direction for Life's Sacred Questions, Sue Monk Kidd, HarperSanFranciso, 1990

The Celestine Prophesy, James Redfield, Warner Books, Inc., 1997

Eat, Pray, Love, Elizabeth Gilbert, Penguin Books, 2006

Teresa of Avila: Selections from the Interior Castle, HarperSanFrancisco, 2004

Silent Spring, Rachel Carson, Houghton Mifflin Company, 1962

1000 Places to See Before You Die, Patricia Schultz, Workman Publishing, 2003

Christy, Catherine Marshall, McGraw-Hill Book Company,1967)

The Artists Way: A Spiritual Path to Higher Creativity, Julia Cameron, Tarcher/Putnam, 1992

Loving What is: Four Questions that Can Change Your Life, Byron Katie, Three Rivers Press, 2002

Teachings of Rumi, Andrew Harvey, Shambhala, 1999

The Naked Now: Learning to See as the Mystics See, Richard Rohr, Crossroads Publishing, 2009

Maureen Hovenkotter graduated from Marylhurst University with a degree in Communications. As a freelance writer, she has published hundreds of articles in newspapers and magazines. In 2007 she retired from her job with the U.S. Senate to embark on this journey. In 2010 she formed Gray Wings Press, LLC, a small, privately held publishing company. She lives near Portland, Oregon, with her golden retriever Charlie who misses sitting on the dashboard of the Mo but likes having his own yard again.